THE HOLY RULE OF ST. BENEDICT:

REGULA SANCITSSIMI PATRIS BENEDICTI

IN ENGLISH AND LATIN

VERITATIS SPLENDOR PUBLICATIONS

et cognoscetis veritatem et veritas liberabit vos (Jn 8:32)

MMXIV

The English text of this book is excerpted from:

The Holy Rule of St. Benedict
The 1949 Edition
Translated by Rev. Boniface Verheyen, OSB of St.
Benedict's Abbey, Atchison, Kansas
The Latin text is from the original.

The English and Latin text of this work is in the public domain.

Retypeset and republished in 2014 by Veritatis Splendor Publications.

AD MAJOREM DEI GLORIAM

CONTENTS

THE HOLY RULE
OF
ST. BENEDICT

PROLOGUE

Listen, O my son, to the precepts of thy master, and incline the ear of thy heart, and cheerfully receive and faithfully execute the admonitions of thy loving Father, that by the toil of obedience thou mayest return to Him from whom by the sloth of disobedience thou hast gone away.

To thee, therefore, my speech is now directed, who, giving up thine own will, takest up the strong and most excellent arms of obedience, to do battle for Christ the Lord, the true King.

In the first place, beg of Him by most earnest prayer, that He perfect whatever good thou dost begin, in order that He who hath been pleased to count us in the number of His children, need never be grieved at our evil deeds. For we ought at all times so to serve Him with the good things which He hath given us, that He may not, like an angry father, disinherit his children, nor, like a dread lord, enraged at our evil deeds, hand us over to everlasting punishment as most wicked servants, who would not follow Him to glory.

Let us then rise at length, since the Scripture arouseth us, saying: "It is now the hour for us to rise from sleep" (Rom 13:11); and having opened our eyes to the deifying light, let us hear with awestruck ears what the divine voice, crying out daily, doth admonish us, saying: "Today, if you shall hear his voice, harden not your hearts" (Ps 94[95]:8). And again: "He that hath ears to hear let him hear what the Spirit saith to the churches" (Rev 2:7). And what doth He say? -- "Come, children, hearken unto me, I will teach you the fear of the Lord" (Ps 33[34]:12). "Run whilst you have the light of life, that the darkness of death overtake you not" (Jn 12:35).

And the Lord seeking His workman in the multitude of the people, to whom He proclaimeth these words, saith again: "Who is the man that desireth life and loveth to see good days" (Ps 33[34]:13)? If hearing this thou answerest, "I am he," God saith to thee: "If thou wilt have true and everlasting life, keep thy tongue from evil, and thy lips from speaking guile; turn away from evil and do good; seek after peace and pursue it" (Ps 33[34]:14-15). And when you shall have done these things, my eyes shall be upon you, and my ears unto your prayers. And before you shall call upon me I will say: "Behold, I am here" (Is 58:9).

What, dearest brethren, can be sweeter to us than this voice of the Lord inviting us? See, in His loving kindness, the Lord showeth us the way of life. Therefore, having our loins girt with faith and the performance of good works, let us walk His ways under the guidance of the Gospel, that we may be found worthy of seeing Him who hath called us to His kingdom (cf 1 Thes 2:12).

If we desire to dwell in the tabernacle of His kingdom, we cannot reach it in any way, unless we run thither by good works. But let us ask the Lord with the Prophet, saying to Him: "Lord, who shall dwell in Thy tabernacle, or who shall rest in Thy holy hill" (Ps 14[15]:1)?

After this question, brethren, let us listen to the Lord answering and showing us the way to this tabernacle, saying: "He that walketh without blemish and worketh justice; he that speaketh truth in his heart; who hath not used deceit in his tongue, nor hath done evil to his neighbor, nor hath taken up a reproach against his neighbor" (Ps 14[15]:2-3), who hath brought to naught the foul demon tempting him, casting him out of his heart with his temptation, and hath taken his evil thoughts whilst they were yet weak and hath dashed them against Christ (cf Ps 14[15]:4; Ps 136[137]:9); who fearing the Lord are not puffed up by their goodness of life, but holding that the actual good which is in them cannot be done by themselves, but by the Lord, they praise the Lord working in them (cf Ps 14[15]:4), saying with the Prophet: "Not to us, O Lord, not to us; by to Thy name give glory" (Ps 113[115:1]:9). Thus also the Apostle Paul hath not taken to himself any credit for his preaching, saying: "By the grace of God, I am what I am" (1 Cor 15:10). And again he saith: "He that glorieth, let him glory in the Lord" (2 Cor 10:17).

Hence, the Lord also saith in the Gospel: "He that heareth these my words and doeth them, shall be likened to a wise man who built his house upon a rock; the floods came, the winds blew, and they beat upon that house, and it fell not, for it was founded on a rock" (Mt 7:24-25). The Lord fulfilling these words waiteth for us from day to day, that we respond to His holy admonitions by our works. Therefore, our days are lengthened to a truce for the amendment of the misdeeds of our present life; as the Apostle saith: "Knowest thou not that the patience of God leadeth thee to penance" (Rom 2:4)? For the good Lord saith: "I will not the death of the sinner, but that he be converted and live" (Ezek 33:11).

Now, brethren, that we have asked the Lord who it is that shall dwell in His tabernacle, we have heard the conditions for dwelling there; and if we fulfil the duties of tenants, we shall be heirs of the kingdom of heaven. Our hearts and our bodies must, therefore, be ready to do battle under the biddings of holy obedience; and let us ask the Lord that He supply by the help of His grace what is impossible to us by nature. And if, flying from the pains of hell, we desire to reach life everlasting, then, while there is yet time, and we are still in the flesh, and are able during the present life to fulfil all these things, we must make haste to do now what will profit us forever.

We are, therefore, about to found a school of the Lord's service, in which we hope to introduce nothing harsh or burdensome. But even if, to correct vices or to preserve charity, sound reason dictateth anything that turneth out somewhat stringent, do not at once fly in dismay from the way of salvation, the beginning of which cannot but be narrow. But as we advance in the religious life and faith, we shall run the way of God's commandments with expanded hearts and unspeakable sweetness of love; so that never departing from His guidance and persevering in the monastery in His doctrine till death, we may by patience share in the sufferings of Christ, and be found worthy to be coheirs with Him of His kingdom.

CHAPTER I
Of the Kinds or the Life of Monks

It is well known that there are four kinds of monks. The first kind is that of Cenobites, that is, the monastic, who live under a rule and an Abbot.

The second kind is that of Anchorites, or Hermits, that is, of those who, no longer in the first fervor of their conversion, but taught by long monastic practice and the help of many brethren, have already learned to fight against the devil; and going forth from the rank of their brethren well trained for single combat in the desert, they are able, with the help of God, to cope single-handed without the help of others, against the vices of the flesh and evil thoughts.

But a third and most vile class of monks is that of Sarabaites, who have been tried by no rule under the hand of a master, as gold is tried in the fire (cf Prov 27:21); but, soft as lead, and still keeping faith with the world by their works, they are known to belie God by their tonsure. Living in two's and three's, or even singly, without a shepherd, enclosed, not in the Lord's sheepfold, but in their own, the gratification of their desires is law unto them; because what they choose to do they call holy, but what they dislike they hold to be unlawful.

But the fourth class of monks is that called Landlopers, who keep going their whole life long from one province to another, staying three or four days at a time in different cells as guests. Always roving and never settled, they indulge their passions and the cravings of their appetite, and are in every way worse than the Sarabaites. It is better to pass all these over in silence than to speak of their most wretched life.

Therefore, passing these over, let us go on with the help of God to lay down a rule for that most valiant kind of monks, the Cenobites.

CHAPTER II
What Kind of Man the Abbot Ought to Be

The Abbot who is worthy to be over a monastery, ought always to be mindful of what he is called, and make his works square with his name of Superior. For he is believed to hold the place of Christ in the monastery, when he is called by his name, according to the saying of the Apostle: "You have received the spirit of adoption of sons, whereby we cry *Abba* (Father)" (Rom 8:15). Therefore, the Abbot should never teach, prescribe, or command (which God forbid) anything contrary to the laws of the Lord; but his commands and teaching should be instilled like a leaven of divine justice into the minds of his disciples.

Let the Abbot always bear in mind that he must give an account in the dread judgment of God of both his own teaching and of the obedience of his disciples. And let the Abbot know that whatever lack of profit the master of the house shall find in the sheep, will be laid to the blame of the shepherd. On the other hand he will be blameless, if he gave all a shepherd's care to his restless and unruly flock, and took all pains to correct their corrupt manners; so that their shepherd, acquitted at the Lord's judgment seat, may say to the Lord with the Prophet: "I have not hid Thy justice within my heart. I have declared Thy truth and Thy salvation" (Ps 39[40]:11). "But they contemning have despised me" (Is 1:2; Ezek 20:27). Then at length eternal death will be the crushing doom of the rebellious sheep under his charge.

When, therefore, anyone taketh the name of Abbot he should govern his disciples by a twofold teaching; namely, he should show them all that is good and holy by his deeds more than by his words; explain the commandments of God to intelligent disciples by words, but show the divine precepts to the dull and simple by his works. And let him show by his actions, that whatever he teacheth his disciples as being

contrary to the law of God must not be done,
"lest perhaps when he hath preached to others,
he himself should become a castaway" (1 Cor
9:27), and he himself committing sin, God one
day say to him: "Why dost thou declare My
justices, and take My covenant in thy mouth?
But thou hast hated discipline, and hast cast My
words behind thee" (Ps 49[50]:16-17). And:
"Thou who sawest the mote in thy brother's
eye, hast not seen the beam in thine own" (Mt
7:3).

Let him make no distinction of persons in the
monastery. Let him not love one more than
another, unless it be one whom he findeth more
exemplary in good works and obedience. Let
not a free-born be preferred to a freedman,
unless there be some other reasonable cause.
But if from a just reason the Abbot deemeth it
proper to make such a distinction, he may do so
in regard to the rank of anyone whomsoever;
otherwise let everyone keep his own place; for
whether bond or free, we are all one in Christ
(cf Gal 3:28; Eph 6:8), and we all bear an equal
burden of servitude under one Lord, "for there
is no respect of persons with God" (Rom 2:11).
We are distinguished with Him in this respect
alone, if we are found to excel others in good
works and in humility. Therefore, let him have
equal charity for all, and impose a uniform
discipline for all according to merit.

For in his teaching the Abbot should always observe that principle of the Apostle in which he saith: "Reprove, entreat, rebuke" (2 Tm 4:2), that is, mingling gentleness with severity, as the occasion may call for, let him show the severity of the master and the loving affection of a father. He must sternly rebuke the undisciplined and restless; but he must exhort the obedient, meek, and patient to advance in virtue. But we charge him to rebuke and punish the negligent and haughty. Let him not shut his eyes to the sins of evil-doers; but on their first appearance let him do his utmost to cut them out from the root at once, mindful of the fate of Heli, the priest of Silo (cf 1 Sam 2:11-4:18). The well-disposed and those of good understanding, let him correct at the first and second admonition only with words; but let him chastise the wicked and the hard of heart, and the proud and disobedient at the very first offense with stripes and other bodily punishments, knowing that it is written: "The fool is not corrected with words" (Prov 29:19). And again: "Strike thy son with the rod, and thou shalt deliver his soul from death" (Prov 23:14).

The Abbot ought always to remember what he is and what he is called, and to know that to whom much hath been entrusted, from him much will be required; and let him understand what a difficult and arduous task he assumeth in

governing souls and accommodating himself to
a variety of characters. Let him so adjust and
adapt himself to everyone -- to one gentleness
of speech, to another by reproofs, and to still
another by entreaties, to each one according to
his bent and understanding -- that he not only
suffer no loss in his flock, but may rejoice in the
increase of a worthy fold.

Above all things, that the Abbot may not
neglect or undervalue the welfare of the souls
entrusted to him, let him not have too great a
concern about fleeting, earthly, perishable
things; but let him always consider that he hath
undertaken the government of souls, of which
he must give an account. And that he may not
perhaps complain of the want of earthly means,
let him remember what is written: "Seek ye first
the kingdom of God and His justice, and all
these things shall be added unto you" (Mt 6:33).
And again: "There is no want to them that fear
Him" (Ps 33[34]:10). And let him know that he
who undertaketh the government of souls must
prepare himself to give an account for them;
and whatever the number of brethren he hath
under his charge, let him be sure that on
judgment day he will, without doubt, have to
give an account to the Lord for all these souls,
in addition to that of his own. And thus, whilst
he is in constant fear of the Shepherd's future
examination about the sheep entrusted to him,

and is watchful of his account for others, he is made solicitous also on his own account; and whilst by his admonitions he had administered correction to others, he is freed from his own failings.

CHAPTER III
Of Calling the Brethren for Counsel

Whenever weighty matters are to be transacted in the monastery, let the Abbot call together the whole community, and make known the matter which is to be considered. Having heard the brethren's views, let him weigh the matter with himself and do what he thinketh best. It is for this reason, however, we said that all should be called for counsel, because the Lord often revealeth to the younger what is best. Let the brethren, however, give their advice with humble submission, and let them not presume stubbornly to defend what seemeth right to them, for it must depend rather on the Abbot's will, so that all obey him in what he considereth best. But as it becometh disciples to obey their master, so also it becometh the master to dispose all things with prudence and justice. Therefore, let all follow the Rule as their guide in everything, and let no one rashly depart from it.

Let no one in the monastery follow the bent of his own heart, and let no one dare to dispute insolently with his Abbot, either inside or outside the monastery. If any one dare to do so, let him be placed under the correction of the Rule. Let the Abbot himself, however, do everything in the fear of the Lord and out of reverence for the Rule, knowing that, beyond a doubt, he will have to give an account to God, the most just Judge, for all his rulings. If, however, matters of less importance, having to do with the welfare of the monastery, are to be treated of, let him use the counsel of the Seniors only, as it is written: "Do all things with counsel, and thou shalt not repent when thou hast done" (Sir 32:24).

CHAPTER IV
The Instruments of Good Works

(1) In the first place to love the Lord God with the whole heart, the whole soul, the whole strength...

(2) Then, one's neighbor as one's self (cf Mt 22:37-39; Mk 12:30-31; Lk 10:27).

(3) Then, not to kill...

(4) Not to commit adultery...

(5) Not to steal...

(6) Not to covet (cf Rom 13:9).

(7) Not to bear false witness (cf Mt 19:18; Mk 10:19; Lk 18:20).

(8) To honor all men (cf 1 Pt 2:17).

(9) And what one would not have done to himself, not to do to another (cf Tob 4:16; Mt 7:12; Lk 6:31).

(10) To deny one's self in order to follow Christ (cf Mt 16:24; Lk 9:23).

(11) To chastise the body (cf 1 Cor 9:27).

(12) Not to seek after pleasures.

(13) To love fasting.

(14) To relieve the poor.

(15) To clothe the naked...

(16) To visit the sick (cf Mt 25:36).

(17) To bury the dead.

(18) To help in trouble.

(19) To console the sorrowing.

(20) To hold one's self aloof from worldly ways.

(21) To prefer nothing to the love of Christ.

(22) Not to give way to anger.

(23) Not to foster a desire for revenge.

(24) Not to entertain deceit in the heart.

(25) Not to make a false peace.

(26) Not to forsake charity.

(27) Not to swear, lest perchance one swear falsely.

(28) To speak the truth with heart and tongue.

(29) Not to return evil for evil (cf 1 Thes 5:15; 1 Pt 3:9).

(30) To do no injury, yea, even patiently to bear the injury done us.

(31) To love one's enemies (cf Mt 5:44; Lk 6:27).

(32) Not to curse them that curse us, but rather

to bless them.

(33) To bear persecution for justice sake (cf Mt 5:10).

(34) Not to be proud...

(35) Not to be given to wine (cf Ti 1:7; 1 Tm 3:3).

(36) Not to be a great eater.

(37) Not to be drowsy.

(38) Not to be slothful (cf Rom 12:11).

(39) Not to be a murmurer.

(40) Not to be a detractor.

(41) To put one's trust in God.

(42) To refer what good one sees in himself, not to self, but to God.

(43) But as to any evil in himself, let him be convinced that it is his own and charge it to himself.

(44) To fear the day of judgment.

(45) To be in dread of hell.

(46) To desire eternal life with all spiritual longing.

(47) To keep death before one's eyes daily.

(48) To keep a constant watch over the actions of our life.

(49) To hold as certain that God sees us everywhere.

(50) To dash at once against Christ the evil thoughts which rise in one's heart.

(51) And to disclose them to our spiritual father.

(52) To guard one's tongue against bad and wicked speech.

(53) Not to love much speaking.

(54) Not to speak useless words and such as provoke laughter.

(55) Not to love much or boisterous laughter.

(56) To listen willingly to holy reading.

(57) To apply one's self often to prayer.

(58) To confess one's past sins to God daily in prayer with sighs and tears, and to amend them for the future.

(59) Not to fulfil the desires of the flesh (cf Gal 5:16).

(60) To hate one's own will.

(61) To obey the commands of the Abbot in all things, even though he himself (which Heaven forbid) act otherwise, mindful of that precept of the Lord: "What they say, do ye; what they do, do ye not" (Mt 23:3).

(62) Not to desire to be called holy before one is; but to be holy first, that one may be truly so called.

(63) To fulfil daily the commandments of God by works.

(64) To love chastity.

(65) To hate no one.

(66) Not to be jealous; not to entertain envy.

(67) Not to love strife.

(68) Not to love pride.

(69) To honor the aged.

(70) To love the younger.

(71) To pray for one's enemies in the love of Christ.

(72) To make peace with an adversary before

the setting of the sun.

(73) And never to despair of God's mercy.

Behold, these are the instruments of the spiritual art, which, if they have been applied without ceasing day and night and approved on judgment day, will merit for us from the Lord that reward which He hath promised: "The eye hath not seen, nor the ear heard, neither hath it entered into the heart of man, what things God hath prepared for them that love Him" (1 Cor 2:9). But the workshop in which we perform all these works with diligence is the enclosure of the monastery, and stability in the community.

CHAPTER V
Of Obedience

The first degree of humility is obedience without delay. This becometh those who, on account of the holy subjection which they have promised, or of the fear of hell, or the glory of life everlasting, hold nothing dearer than Christ. As soon as anything hath been commanded by the Superior they permit no delay in the execution, as if the matter had been commanded by God Himself. Of these the Lord saith: "At the hearing of the ear he hath obeyed Me" (Ps 17[18]:45). And again He saith to the teachers: "He that heareth you heareth Me" (Lk 10:16).

Such as these, therefore, instantly quitting their own work and giving up their own will, with hands disengaged, and leaving unfinished what they were doing, follow up, with the ready step of obedience, the work of command with deeds; and thus, as if in the same moment, both matters -- the master's command and the disciple's finished work -- are, in the swiftness of the fear of God, speedily finished together, whereunto the desire of advancing to eternal life urgeth them. They, therefore, seize upon the narrow way whereof the Lord saith: "Narrow is the way which leadeth to life" (Mt 7:14), so that, not living according to their own desires and pleasures but walking according to the judgment and will of another, they live in monasteries, and desire an Abbot to be over them. Such as these truly live up to the maxim of the Lord in which He saith: "I came not to do My own will, but the will of Him that sent Me" (Jn 6:38).

This obedience, however, will be acceptable to God and agreeable to men then only, if what is commanded is done without hesitation, delay, lukewarmness, grumbling or complaint, because the obedience which is rendered to Superiors is rendered to God. For He Himself hath said: "He that heareth you heareth Me" (Lk 10:16). And it must be rendered by the disciples with a good will, "for the Lord loveth a cheerful giver (2 Cor 9:7). " For if the disciple obeyeth with an ill will, and murmureth, not only with lips but also in his heart, even though he fulfil the command, yet it will not be acceptable to God, who regardeth the heart of the murmurer. And for such an action he acquireth no reward; rather he incurreth the penalty of murmurers, unless he maketh satisfactory amendment.

CHAPTER VI
Of Silence

Let us do what the Prophet saith: "I said, I will take heed of my ways, that I sin not with my tongue: I have set a guard to my mouth, I was dumb, and was humbled, and kept silence even from good things" (Ps 38[39]:2-3). Here the prophet showeth that, if at times we ought to refrain from useful speech for the sake of silence, how much more ought we to abstain from evil words on account of the punishment due to sin.

Therefore, because of the importance of silence, let permission to speak be seldom given to perfect disciples even for good and holy and edifying discourse, for it is written: "In much talk thou shalt not escape sin" (Prov 10:19). And elsewhere: "Death and life are in the power of the tongue" (Prov 18:21). For it belongeth to the master to speak and to teach; it becometh the disciple to be silent and to listen. If, therefore, anything must be asked of the Superior, let it be asked with all humility and respectful submission. But coarse jests, and idle words or speech provoking laughter, we condemn everywhere to eternal exclusion; and for such speech we do not permit the disciple to open his lips.

CHAPTER VII
Of Humility

Brethren, the Holy Scripture crieth to us saying: "Every one that exalteth himself shall be humbled; and he that humbleth himself shall be exalted" (Lk 14:11; 18:14). Since, therefore, it saith this, it showeth us that every exaltation is a kind of pride. The Prophet declareth that he guardeth himself against this, saying: "Lord, my heart is not puffed up; nor are my eyes haughty. Neither have I walked in great matters nor in wonderful things above me" (Ps 130[131]:1). What then? "If I was not humbly minded, but exalted my soul; as a child that is weaned is towards his mother so shalt Thou reward my soul" (Ps 130[131]:2).

Hence, brethren, if we wish to reach the greatest height of humility, and speedily to arrive at that heavenly exaltation to which ascent is made in the present life by humility, then, mounting by our actions, we must erect the ladder which appeared to Jacob in his dream, by means of which angels were shown to him ascending and descending (cf Gen 28:12). Without a doubt, we understand this ascending and descending to be nothing else but that we descend by pride and ascend by humility. The erected ladder, however, is our life in the present world, which, if the heart is humble, is by the Lord lifted up to heaven. For we say that our body and our soul are the two sides of this ladder; and into these sides the divine calling hath inserted various degrees of humility or discipline which we must mount.

The first degree of humility, then, is that a man always have the fear of God before his eyes (cf Ps 35[36]:2), shunning all forgetfulness and that he be ever mindful of all that God hath commanded, that he always considereth in his mind how those who despise God will burn in hell for their sins, and that life everlasting is prepared for those who fear God. And whilst he guardeth himself evermore against sin and vices of thought, word, deed, and self-will, let him also hasten to cut off the desires of the flesh.

Let a man consider that God always seeth him from Heaven, that the eye of God beholdeth his works everywhere, and that the angels report them to Him every hour. The Prophet telleth us this when he showeth God thus ever present in our thoughts, saying: "The searcher of hearts and reins is God" (Ps 7:10). And again: "The Lord knoweth the thoughts of men" (Ps 93[94]:11) And he saith: "Thou hast understood my thoughts afar off" (Ps 138[139]:3). And: "The thoughts of man shall give praise to Thee" (Ps 75[76]:11). Therefore, in order that he may always be on his guard against evil thoughts, let the humble brother always say in his heart: "Then I shall be spotless before Him, if I shall keep myself from iniquity" (Ps 17[18]:24).

We are thus forbidden to do our own will, since the Scripture saith to us: "And turn away from thy evil will" (Sir 18:30). And thus, too, we ask God in prayer that His will may be done in us (cf Mt 6:10). We are, therefore, rightly taught not to do our own will, when we guard against what Scripture saith: "There are ways that to men seem right, the end whereof plungeth into the depths of hell" (Prov 16:25). And also when we are filled with dread at what is said of the negligent: "They are corrupted and become abominable in their pleasure" (Ps 13[14]:1). But as regards desires of the flesh, let us believe that God is thus ever present to us, since the Prophet saith to the Lord: "Before Thee is all my desire" (Ps 37[38]:10).

We must, therefore, guard thus against evil desires, because death hath his station near the entrance of pleasure. Whence the Scripture commandeth, saying: "Go no after thy lusts" (Sir 18:30). If, therefore, the eyes of the Lord observe the good and the bad (cf Prov 15:3) and the Lord always looketh down from heaven on the children of men, to see whether there be anyone that understandeth or seeketh God (cf Ps 13[14]:2); and if our actions are reported to the Lord day and night by the angels who are appointed to watch over us daily, we must ever be on our guard, brethren, as the Prophet saith in the psalm, that God may at no time see us "gone aside to evil and become unprofitable" (Ps 13[14]:3), and having spared us in the present time, because He is kind and waiteth for us to be changed for the better, say to us in the future: "These things thou hast done and I was silent" (Ps 49[50]:21).

The second degree of humility is, when a man loveth not his own will, nor is pleased to fulfill his own desires but by his deeds carrieth our that word of the Lord which saith: "I came not to do My own will but the will of Him that sent Me" (Jn 6:38). It is likewise said: "Self-will hath its punishment, but necessity winneth the crown."

The third degree of humility is, that for the love of God a man subject himself to a Superior in all obedience, imitating the Lord, of whom the Apostle saith: "He became obedient unto death" (Phil 2:8).

The fourth degree of humility is, that, if hard and distasteful things are commanded, nay, even though injuries are inflicted, he accept them with patience and even temper, and not grow weary or give up, but hold out, as the Scripture saith: "He that shall persevere unto the end shall be saved" (Mt 10:22). And again: "Let thy heart take courage, and wait thou for the Lord" (Ps 26[27]:14). And showing that a faithful man ought even to bear every disagreeable thing for the Lord, it saith in the person of the suffering: "For Thy sake we suffer death all the day long; we are counted as sheep for the slaughter" (Rom 8:36; Ps 43[44]:22). And secure in the hope of the divine reward, they go on joyfully, saying: "But in all these things we overcome because of Him that hath loved us" (Rom 8:37). And likewise in another place the Scripture saith: "Thou, O God, hast proved us; Thou hast tried us by fire as silver is tried; Thou hast brought us into a net, Thou hast laid afflictions on our back" (Ps 65[66]:10-11). And to show us that we ought to be under a Superior, it continueth, saying: "Thou hast set men over our heads" (Ps 65[66]:12). And fulfilling the command of the Lord by patience also in adversities and injuries, when struck on the one cheek they turn also the other; the despoiler of their coat they give their cloak also; and when forced to go one mile they go two (cf Mt 5:39-41); with the Apostle Paul they bear with false brethren and "bless those who curse them" (2 Cor 11:26; 1 Cor 4:12).

The fifth degree of humility is, when one hideth from his Abbot none of the evil thoughts which rise in his heart or the evils committed by him in secret, but humbly confesseth them. Concerning this the Scripture exhorts us, saying: "Reveal thy way to the Lord and trust in Him" (Ps 36[37]:5). And it saith further: "Confess to the Lord, for He is good, for His mercy endureth forever" (Ps 105[106]:1; Ps 117[118]:1). And the Prophet likewise saith: "I have acknowledged my sin to Thee and my injustice I have not concealed. I said I will confess against myself my injustice to the Lord; and Thou hast forgiven the wickedness of my sins" (Ps 31[32]:5).

The sixth degree of humility is, when a monk is content with the meanest and worst of everything, and in all that is enjoined him holdeth himself as a bad and worthless workman, saying with the Prophet: "I am brought to nothing and I knew it not; I am become as a beast before Thee, and I am always with Thee" (Ps 72[73]:22-23).

The seventh degree of humility is, when, not only with his tongue he declareth, but also in his inmost soul believeth, that he is the lowest and vilest of men, humbling himself and saying with the Prophet: "But I am a worm and no man, the reproach of men and the outcast of the people" (Ps 21[22]:7). "I have been exalted and humbled and confounded" (Ps 87[88]:16). And also: "It is good for me that Thou hast humbled me, that I may learn Thy commandments" (Ps 118[119]:71,73).

The eighth degree of humility is, when a monk doeth nothing but what is sanctioned by the common rule of the monastery and the example of his elders.

The ninth degree of humility is, when a monk withholdeth his tongue from speaking, and keeping silence doth not speak until he is asked; for the Scripture showeth that "in a multitude of words there shall not want sin" (Prov 10:19); and that "a man full of tongue is not established in the earth" (Ps 139[140]:12).

The tenth degree of humility is, when a monk is not easily moved and quick for laughter, for it is written: "The fool exalteth his voice in laughter" (Sir 21:23).

The eleventh degree of humility is, that, when a monk speaketh, he speak gently and without laughter, humbly and with gravity, with few and sensible words, and that he be not loud of voice, as it is written: "The wise man is known by the fewness of his words."

The twelfth degree of humility is, when a monk is not only humble of heart, but always letteth it appear also in his whole exterior to all that see him; namely, at the Work of God, in the garden, on a journey, in the field, or wherever he may be, sitting, walking, or standing, let him always have his head bowed down, his eyes fixed on the ground, ever holding himself guilty of his sins, thinking that he is already standing before the dread judgment seat of God, and always saying to himself in his heart what the publican in the Gospel said, with his eyes fixed on the ground: "Lord, I am a sinner and not worthy to lift up mine eyes to heaven" (Lk 18:13); and again with the Prophet: "I am bowed down and humbled exceedingly" (Ps 37[38]:7-9; Ps 118[119]:107).

Having, therefore, ascended all these degrees of humility, the monk will presently arrive at that love of God, which being perfect, casteth out

fear (1 Jn 4:18). In virtue of this love all things
which at first he observed not without fear, he
will now begin to keep without any effort, and
as it were, naturally by force of habit, no longer
from the fear of hell, but from the love of
Christ, from the very habit of good and the
pleasure in virtue. May the Lord be pleased to
manifest all this by His Holy Spirit in His
laborer now cleansed from vice and sin.

CHAPTER VIII
Of the Divine Office during the Night

Making due allowance for circumstances, the
brethren will rise during the winter season, that
is, from the calends of November till Easter, at
the eighth hour of the night; so that, having
rested till a little after midnight, they may rise
refreshed. The time, however, which remains
over after the night office (Matins) will be
employed in study by those of the brethren who
still have some parts of the psalms and the
lessons to learn.

But from Easter to the aforesaid calends, let the
hour for celebrating the night office (Matins) be
so arranged, that after a very short interval,
during which the brethren may go out for the
necessities of nature, the morning office
(Lauds), which is to be said at the break of day,
may follow presently.

CHAPTER IX

How Many Psalms Are to Be Said at the Night Office

During the winter season, having in the first place said the verse: *Deus, in adjutorium meum intende; Domine, ad adjuvandum me festina*, there is next to be said three times, *Domine, labia mea aperies, et os meum annuntiabit laudem tuam* (Ps 50[51]:17). To this the third psalm and the *Gloria* are to be added. After this the 94th psalm with its antiphon is to be said or chanted. Hereupon let a hymn follow, and after that six psalms with antiphons. When these and the verse have been said, let the Abbot give the blessing. All being seated on the benches, let three lessons be read alternately by the brethren from the book on the reading stand, between which let three responsories be said. Let two of the responsories be said without the *Gloria*, but after the third lesson, let him who is chanting say the *Gloria*. When the cantor beginneth to sing it, let all rise at once from their seats in honor and reverence of the Blessed Trinity.

Let the inspired books of both the Old and the New Testaments be read at the night offices, as also the expositions of them which have been made by the most eminent orthodox and Catholic Fathers.

After these three lessons with their responsories, let six other psalms follow, to be sung with *Alleluia*. After these let the lessons from the Apostle follow, to be said by heart, then the verse, the invocation of the litany, that is, *Kyrie eleison*. And thus let the night office come to an end.

CHAPTER X
How the Office Is to Be Said during the Summer Season

From Easter till the calends of November let the whole psalmody, as explained above, be said, except that on account of the shortness of the nights, no lessons are read from the book; but instead of these three lessons, let one from the Old Testament be said from memory. Let a short responsory follow this, and let all the rest be performed as was said; namely, that never fewer than twelve psalms be said at the night office, exclusive of the third and the 94th psalm.

CHAPTER XI
How the Night Office Is to Be Said on Sundays

For the night office on Sunday the monks should rise earlier. At this office let the following regulations be observed, namely: after six psalms and the verse have been sung, as we arranged above, and all have been properly seated on the benches in their order, let four lessons with their responsories be read from the book, as we said above. In the fourth responsory only, let the *Gloria* be said by the chanter, and as soon as he beginneth it let all presently rise with reverence.

After these lessons let six other psalms with antiphons and the verse follow in order as before. After these let there be said three canticles from the Prophets, selected by the Abbot, and chanted with *Alleluia*. When the verse also hath been said and the Abbot hath given the blessing, let four other lessons from the New Testament be read in the order above mentioned. But after the fourth responsory let the Abbot intone the hymn *Te Deum laudamus*. When this hath been said, let the Abbot read the lesson from the Gospel, all standing with reverence and awe. When the Gospel hath been read let all answer *Amen*, and immediately the Abbot will follow up with the hymn *Te decet laus*, and when he hath given the blessing Lauds will begin.

Let this order of the night office be observed on Sunday the same way in all seasons, in summer as well as in winter, unless perchance (which God forbid) the brethren should rise too late and part of the lessons or the responsories would have to be shortened. Let every precaution be taken that this does not occur. If it should happen, let him through whose neglect it came about make due satisfaction for it to God in the oratory.

CHAPTER XII
How Lauds Are to Be Said

At Lauds on Sunday, let the 66th psalm be said first simply, without an antiphon. After that let the 50th psalm be said with *Alleluia*; after this let the 117th and the 62d be said; then the blessing and the praises, one lesson from the Apocalypse, said by heart, a responsory, the Ambrosian hymn, the verse and the canticle from the Gospel, the litany, and it is finished.

CHAPTER XIII
How Lauds Are to Be Said on Week Days

On week days let Lauds be celebrated in the following manner, to wit: Let the 66th psalm be said without an antiphon, drawing it out a little as on Sunday, that all may arriver for the 50th, which is to be said with an antiphon. After this let two other psalms be said according to custom; namely, the 5th and the 35th on the second day, the 42d and the 56th on the third day, the 63rd and the 64th on the fourth day, the 87th and the 89th on the fifth day, the 75th and the 91st on the sixth day, and on Saturday the 142d and the canticle of Deuteronomy, which should be divided into two *Glorias*. On the other days, however, let the canticle from the Prophets, each for its proper day, be said as the Roman Church singeth it. After these let the psalms of praise follow; then one lesson from the Apostle, to be said from memory, the responsory, the Ambrosian hymn, the verse, the canticle from the Gospel, the litany, and it is finished.

Owing to the sandals which are wont to spring up, the morning and the evening office should, plainly, never end unless the Lord's Prayer is said in the hearing of all by the Superior in its place at the end; so that in virtue of the promise which the brethren make when they say, "Forgive us as we forgive" (Mt 6:12), they may cleanse themselves of failings of this kind.

At the other hours which are to be said, however, let only the last part of this prayer be said aloud, so that all may answer, "But deliver us from evil" (Mt 6:13).

CHAPTER XIV

How the Night Office Is to Be Said on the Feasts of the Saints

On the feasts of the saints and on all solemn festivals let the night office be performed as we said it should be done on Sunday; except that the psalms, the antiphons, and the lessons proper for that day be said; but let the number above mentioned be maintained.

CHAPTER XV

At What Times the Alleluia Is to Be Said

From holy Easter until Pentecost let the *Alleluia* be said without intermission, both with the psalms and with the responsories; but from Pentecost until the beginning of Lent let it be said every night at the nocturns with the six latter psalms only. However, on all Sundays outside of Lent, let the canticles, Lauds, Prime, Tierce, Sext, and None be said with *Alleluia*. Let Vespers, however, be said with the antiphon; but let the responsories never be said with *Alleluia*, except from Easter to Pentecost.

CHAPTER XVI

How the Work of God Is to Be Performed during the Day

As the Prophet saith: "Seven times a day I have given praise to Thee" (Ps 118[119]:164), this sacred sevenfold number will be fulfilled by us in this wise if we perform the duties of our service at the time of Lauds, Prime, Tierce, Sext, None, Vespers, and Complin; because it was of these day hours that he hath said: "Seven times a day I have given praise to Thee" (Ps 118[119]:164). For the same Prophet saith of the night watches: "At midnight I arose to confess to Thee" (Ps 118[119]:62). At these times, therefore, let us offer praise to our Creator "for the judgments of His justice;" namely, at Lauds, Prime, Tierce, Sext, None, Vespers, and Complin; and let us rise at night to praise Him (cf Ps 118[119]:164, 62).

CHAPTER XVII

How Many Psalms Are to Be Sung at These Hours

We have now arranged the order of the psalmody for the night and the morning office; let us next arrange for the succeeding Hours. At the first Hour let three psalms be said separately, and not under one *Gloria*. Let the hymn for the same Hour be said after the verse *Deus, in adjutorium* (Ps 69[70]:2), before the psalms are begun. Then, after the completion of three psalms, let one lesson be said, a verse, the *Kyrie eleison*, and the collects.

At the third, the sixth, and the ninth Hours, the prayer will be said in the same order; namely, the verse, the hymn proper to each Hour, the three psalms, the lesson, the verse, the *Kyrie eleison*, and the collects. If the brotherhood is large, let these Hours be sung with antiphons; but if small, let them be said without a break.

Let the office of Vespers be ended with four psalms and antiphons; after these psalms a lesson is to be recited, next a responsory, the Ambrosian hymn, a verse, the canticle from the Gospel, the litany, the Lord's Prayer, and the collects.

Let Complin end with the saying of three psalms, which are to be said straight on without an antiphon, and after these the hymn for the same Hour, one lesson, the verse, *Kyrie eleison*, the blessing, and the collects.

CHAPTER XVIII
In What Order the Psalms Are to Be Said

In the beginning let there be said the verse, *Deus, in adjutorium meum intende; Domine, ad adjuvandum me festina* (Ps 69[70]:2), and the *Gloria*, followed by the hymn for each Hour. At Prime on Sunday, then, there are to be said four sections of the 118th psalm. At the other Hours, however, namely Tierce, Sext, and None, let three sections of the same psalm be said. But at Prime on Monday let three psalms be said, namely, the first, the second, and the sixth; and thus each day at Prime until Sunday, let three psalms be said each time in consecutive order up to the 19th psalm, yet so that the ninth psalm and the 17th be each divided into two *Glorias*; and thus it will come about that at the night office on Sundays we always begin with the 20th psalm.

At Tierce, Sext, and None, on Monday, however, let the nine sections which remain over the 118th psalm be said, three sections at each of these Hours. The 118th psalm having thus been parceled out for two days, namely, Sunday and Monday, let there be sung on Tuesday for Tierce, Sext, and None, three psalms each, from the 119th to the 127th, that is, nine psalms. These psalms will always be repeated at the same Hours in just the same way until Sunday, observing also for all these days a regular succession of the hymns, the lessons, and the verses, so, namely, that on Sunday the beginning is always made with the 118th psalm.

Let Vespers be sung daily with the singing of four psalms. Let these psalms begin with the 109th to the 147th, excepting those which are set aside for the other Hours; namely, from the 117th to the 127th, and the 133d, and the 142d. All the rest are to be said at Vespers; and as the psalms fall three short, those of the aforesaide psalms which are found to be longer, are to be divided; namely, the 138th, the 143d, and the 144th. But because the 116th is short, let it be joined to the 115th. The order of the psalms for Vespers having thus been arranged let the rest, namely, the lessons, the responsories, the hymns, the verses, and the canticles, be said as we have directed above.

At Complin, however, let the same psalms be repeated every day; namely, the 4th, the 90th, and the 133d.

Having arranged the order of the office, let all the rest of the psalms which remain over, be divided equally into seven night offices, by so dividing such of them as are of greater length that twelve fall to each night. We especially impress this, that, if this distribution of the psalms should perchance displease anyone, he arrange them if he thinketh another better, by all means seeing to it that the whole Psalter of one hundred and fifty psalms be said every week, and that it always start again from the beginning at Matins on Sunday; because those monks show too lax a service in their devotion who in the course of a week chant less than the whole Psalter with is customary canticles; since we read, that our holy forefathers promptly fulfilled in one day what we lukewarm monks should, please God, perform at least in a week.

CHAPTER XIX
Of the Manner of Reciting the Psalter

We believe that God is present everywhere and that the eyes of the Lord behold the good and the bad in every place (cf Prov 15:3). Let us firmly believe this, especially when we take part in the Work of God. Let us, therefore, always be mindful of what the Prophet saith, "Serve ye the Lord with fear" (Ps 2:11). And again, "Sing ye wisely" (Ps 46[47]:8). And, "I will sing praise to Thee in the sight of the angels" (Ps 137[138]:1). Therefore, let us consider how it becometh us to behave in the sight of God and His angels, and let us so stand to sing, that our mind may be in harmony with our voice.

CHAPTER XX
Of Reverence at Prayer

If we do not venture to approach men who are in power, except with humility and reverence, when we wish to ask a favor, how much must we beseech the Lord God of all things with all humility and purity of devotion? And let us be assured that it is not in many words, but in the purity of heart and tears of compunction that we are heard. For this reason prayer ought to be short and pure, unless, perhaps it is lengthened by the inspiration of divine grace. At the community exercises, however, let the prayer always be short, and the sign having been given by the Superior, let all rise together.

CHAPTER XXI
Of the Deans of the Monastery

If the brotherhood is large, let brethren of good repute and holy life be chosen from among them and be appointed Deans; and let them take care of their deaneries in everything according to the commandments of God and the directions of their Abbot. Let such be chosen Deans as the Abbot may safely trust to share his burden. Let them not be chosen for their rank, but for the merit of their life and their wisdom and knowledge; and if any of them, puffed up with pride, should be found blameworthy and, after having been corrected once and again and even a third time, refuseth to amend, let him be deposed, and one who is worthy be placed in his stead. We make the same regulation with reference to the Prior.

CHAPTER XXII
How the Monks Are to Sleep

Let the brethren sleep singly, each in a separate bed. Let them receive the bedding befitting their mode of life, according to the direction of their Abbot. If it can be done, let all sleep in one apartment; but if the number doth not allow it, let them sleep in tens or twenties with the seniors who have charge of them. Let a light be kept burning constantly in the cell till morning.

Let them sleep clothed and girded with cinctures or cords, that they may be always ready; but let them not have knives at their sides whilst they sleep, lest perchance the sleeping be wounded in their dreams; and the sign having been given, rising without delay, let them hasten to outstrip each other to the Work of God, yet with all gravity and decorum. Let the younger brethren not have their beds beside each other, but intermingled with the older ones; and rising to the Work of God, let them gently encourage one another on account of the excuses of the drowsy.

CHAPTER XXIII
Of Excommunication for Faults

If a brother is found stubborn or disobedient or proud or murmuring, or opposed to anything in the Holy Rule and a contemner of the commandments of his Superiors, let him be admonished by his Superiors once and again in secret, according to the command of our Lord (cf Mt 18:15-16). If he doth not amend let him be taken to task publicly before all. But if he doth not reform even then, and he understandeth what a penalty it is, let him be placed under excommunication; but if even then he remaineth obstinate let him undergo corporal punishment.

CHAPTER XXIV
What the Manner of Excommunication Should Be

The degree of excommunication or punishment ought to be meted out according to the gravity of the offense, and to determine that is left to the judgment of the Abbot. If, however, anyone of the brethren is detected in smaller faults, let him be debarred from eating at the common table.

The following shall be the practice respecting one who is excluded from the common table:

that he does not intone a psalm or an antiphon nor read a lesson in the oratory until he hath made satisfaction; let him take his meal alone, after the refection of the brethren; thus: if, for instance, the brethren take their meal at the sixth hour that brother will take his at the ninth, and if the brethren take theirs at the ninth, he will take his in the evening, until by due satisfaction he obtaineth pardon.

CHAPTER XXV
Of Graver Faults

But let the brother who is found guilty of a graver fault be excluded from both the table and the oratory. Let none of the brethren join his company or speak with him. Let him be alone at the work enjoined on him, persevering in penitential sorrow, mindful of the terrible sentence of the Apostle who saith, that "such a man is delivered over for the destruction of the flesh, that the spirit may be saved in the day of the Lord" (1 Cor 5:5). Let him get his food alone in such quantity and at such a time as the Abbot shall deem fit; and let him not be blessed by anyone passing by, nor the food that is given him.

CHAPTER XXVI
Of Those Who without the Command of the Abbot Associate with the Excommunicated

If any brother presume to associate with an excommunicated brother in any way, or to speak with him, or to send him a message, without the command of the Abbot, let him incur the same penalty of excommunication.

CHAPTER XXVII
How Concerned the Abbot Should Be about the Excommunicated

Let the Abbot show all care and concern towards offending brethren because "they that are in health need not a physician, but they that are sick" (Mt 9:12). Therefore, like a prudent physician he ought to use every opportunity to send consolers, namely, discreet elderly brethren, to console the wavering brother, as it were, in secret, and induce him to make humble satisfaction; and let them cheer him up "lest he be swallowed up with overmuch sorrow" (2 Cor 2:7); but, as the same Apostle saith, "confirm your charity towards him" (2 Cor 2:8); and let prayer be said for him by all.

The Abbot must take the utmost pains, and strive with all prudence and zeal, that none of the flock entrusted to him perish. For the Abbot must know that he has taken upon himself the care of infirm souls, not a despotism over the strong; and let him fear the threat of the Prophet wherein the Lord saith: "What ye saw to be fat, that ye took to yourselves, and what was diseased you threw away" (Ezek 34:3-4). And let him follow the loving example of the Good Shepherd, who, leaving the ninety-nine sheep on the mountains, went to seek the one that had gone astray, on whose weakness He had such pity, that He was pleased to lay it on His sacred shoulders and thus carry it back to the fold (cf Lk 15:5).

CHAPTER XXVIII
Of Those Who Having Often Been Corrected Do Not Amend

If a brother hath often been corrected and hath even been excommunicated for a fault and doth not amend, let a more severe correction be applied to him, namely, proceed against him with corporal punishment.

But if even then he doth not reform, or puffed up with pride, should perhaps, which God forbid, even defend his actions, then let the Abbot act like a prudent physician. After he hath applied soothing lotions, ointments of admonitions, medicaments of the Holy

Scriptures, and if, as a last resource, he hath employed the caustic of excommunication and the blows of the lash, and seeth that even then his pains are of no avail, let him apply for that brother also what is more potent than all these measures: his own prayer and that of the brethren, that the Lord who is all-powerful may work a cure in that brother.

But if he is not healed even in this way, then finally let the Abbot dismiss him from the community, as the Apostle saith: "Put away the evil one from among you" (1 Cor 5:13); and again: "If the faithless depart, let him depart" (1 Cor 7:15); lest one diseased sheep infect the whole flock.

CHAPTER XXIX
Whether Brethren Who Leave the Monastery Ought to Be Received Again

If a brother, who through his own fault leaveth the monastery or is expelled, desireth to return, let him first promise full amendment of the fault for which he left; and thus let him be received in the last place, that by this means his humility may be tried. If he should leave again, let him be received even a third time, knowing that after this every means of return will be denied him.

CHAPTER XXX

How Young Boys Are to Be Corrected

Every age and understanding should have its proper discipline. Whenever, therefore, boys or immature youths or such as can not understand how grave a penalty excommunication is, are guilty of a serious fault, let them undergo severe fasting or be disciplined with corporal punishment, that they may be corrected.

CHAPTER XXXI

The Kind of Man the Cellarer of the Monastery Ought to Be

Let there be chosen from the brotherhood as Cellarer of the monastery a wise man, of settled habits, temperate and frugal, not conceited, irritable, resentful, sluggish, or wasteful, but fearing God, who may be as a father to the whole brotherhood.

Let him have the charge of everything, let him do nothing without the command of the Abbot, let him do what hath been ordered him and not grieve the brethren. If a brother should perchance request anything of him unreasonably let him not sadden the brother with a cold refusal, but politely and with humility refuse him who asketh amiss. Let him be watchful of his own soul, always mindful of the saying of the Apostle: "For they that have ministered well, shall purchase to themselves a good degree" (1 Tm 3:13). Let him provide for the sick, the children, the guests, and the poor, with all care, knowing that, without doubt, he will have to give an account of all these things on judgment day. Let him regard all the vessels of the monastery and all its substance, as if they were sacred vessels of the altar. Let him neglect nothing and let him not give way to avarice, nor let him be wasteful and a squanderer of the goods of the monastery; but let him do all things in due measure and according to the bidding of his Abbot.

Above all things, let him be humble; and if he hath not the things to give, let him answer with a kind word, because it is written: "A good word is above the best gift" (Sir 18:17). Let him have under his charge everything that the Abbot hath entrusted to him, and not presume to meddle with matters forbidden him. Let him give the brethren their apportioned allowance without a ruffle or delay, that they may not be scandalized, mindful of what the Divine Word declareth that he deserveth who shall scandalize one of these little ones: "It were better for him that a millstone were hanged about his neck and that he were drowned in the depth of the sea" (Mt 18:6).

If the community is large, let assistants be given him, that, with their help, he too may fulfil the office entrusted to him with an even temper. Let the things that are to be given be distributed, and the things that are to be gotten asked for at the proper times, so that nobody may be disturbed or grieved in the house of God.

CHAPTER XXXII
Of the Tools and Goods of the Monastery

Let the Abbot appoint brethren on whose life and character he can rely, over the property of the monastery in tools, clothing, and things generally, and let him assign to them, as he shall deem proper, all the articles which must be collected after use and stored away. Let the Abbot keep a list of these articles, so that, when the brethren in turn succeed each other in these trusts, he may know what he giveth and what he receiveth back. If anyone, however, handleth the goods of the monastery slovenly or carelessly let him be reprimanded and if he doth not amend let him come under the discipline of the Rule.

CHAPTER XXXIII
Whether Monks Ought to Have Anything of Their Own

The vice of personal ownership must by all means be cut out in the monastery by the very root, so that no one may presume to give or receive anything without the command of the Abbot; nor to have anything whatever as his own, neither a book, nor a writing tablet, nor a pen, nor anything else whatsoever, since monks are allowed to have neither their bodies nor their wills in their own power. Everything that is necessary, however, they must look for from the Father of the monastery; and let it not be allowed for anyone to have anything which the Abbot did not give or permit him to have. Let all things be common to all, as it is written. And let no one call or take to himself anything as his own (cf Acts 4:32). But if anyone should be found to indulge this most baneful vice, and, having been admonished once and again, doth not amend, let him be subjected to punishment.

CHAPTER XXXIV
Whether All Should Receive in Equal Measure What Is Necessary

It is written, "Distribution was made to everyone according as he had need" (Acts 4:35).

We do not say by this that respect should be had for persons (God forbid), but regard for infirmities. Let him who hath need of less thank God and not give way to sadness, but let him who hath need of more, humble himself for his infirmity, and not be elated for the indulgence shown him; and thus all the members will be at peace.

Above all, let not the evil of murmuring appear in the least word or sign for any reason whatever. If anyone be found guilty herein, let him be placed under very severe discipline.

CHAPTER XXXV
Of the Weekly Servers in the Kitchen

Let the brethren serve each other so that no one be excused from the work in the kitchen, except on account of sickness or more necessary work, because greater merit and more charity is thereby acquired. Let help be given to the weak, however, that they may not do this work with sadness; but let all have help according to the size of the community and the circumstances of the place. If the community is large, let the Cellarer be excused from the kitchen, or if, as we have said, any are engaged in more urgent work; let the rest serve each other in charity.

Let him who is to go out of the weekly service, do the cleaning on Saturday. Let him wash the towels with which the brethren wipe their hands and feet. Let him who goeth out, as well as him who is to come in, wash the feet of all. Let him return the utensils of his department to the Cellarer clean and whole. Let the Cellarer give the same to the one who cometh in, so that he may know what he giveth and what he receiveth back.

An hour before meal time let the weekly servers receive each a cup of drink and a piece of bread over the prescribed portion, that they may serve their brethren at the time time of refection without murmuring and undue strain. On solemn feast days, however, let them abstain till after Mass.

As soon as the morning office on Sunday is ended, let the weekly servers who come in and who go out, cast themselves upon their knees in the oratory before all, asking their prayers. Let him who goeth out of the weekly service, say the following verse: *Benedictus es, Domine Deus, qui adjuvisti me et consolatus se me* (Dan 3:52; Ps 85[86]:17). The one going out having said this three times and received the blessing, let the one who cometh in follow and say: *Deus in adjutorium meum intende; Domine, ad adjuvandum me festina* (Ps 69[70]:2). And let this also be repeated three times by all, and having received the blessing let him enter upon his weekly service.

CHAPTER XXXVI
Of the Sick Brethren

Before and above all things, care must be taken of the sick, that they be served in very truth as Christ is served; because He hath said, "I was sick and you visited Me" (Mt 25:36). And "As long as you did it to one of these My least brethren, you did it to Me" (Mt 25:40). But let the sick themselves also consider that they are served for the honor of God, and let them not grieve their brethren who serve them by unnecessary demands. These must, however, be patiently borne with, because from such as these a more bountiful reward is gained. Let the Abbot's greatest concern, therefore, be that they suffer no neglect.

Let a cell be set apart for the sick brethren, and a God-fearing, diligent, and careful attendant be appointed to serve them. Let the use of the bath be offered to the sick as often as it is useful, but let it be granted more rarely to the healthy and especially the young. Thus also let the use of meat be granted to the sick and to the very weak for their recovery. But when they have been restored let them all abstain from meat in the usual manner.

But let the Abbot exercise the utmost care that the sick are not neglected by the Cellarer or the attendants, because whatever his disciples do amiss falleth back on him.

CHAPTER XXXVII
Of the Aged and Children

Although human nature is of itself drawn to feel compassion for these life-periods, namely, old age and childhood, still, let the decree of the Rule make provision also for them. Let their natural weakness be always taken into account and let the strictness of the Rule not be kept with them in respect to food, but let there be a tender regard in their behalf and let them eat before regular hours.

CHAPTER XXXVIII
Of the Weekly Reader

Reading must not be wanting at the table of the brethren when they are eating. Neither let anyone who may chance to take up the book venture to read there; but let him who is to read for the whole week enter upon that office on Sunday. After Mass and Communion let him ask all to pray for him that God may ward off from him the spirit of pride. And let the following verse be said three times by all in the oratory, he beginning it: *Domine, labia mea aperies, et os meum annuntiabit laudem tuam* (Ps 50[51]:17), and thus having received the blessing let him enter upon the reading.

Let the deepest silence be maintained that no whispering or voice be heard except that of the reader alone. But let the brethren so help each other to what is needed for eating and drinking, that no one need ask for anything. If, however, anything should be wanted, let it be asked for by means of a sign of any kind rather than a sound. And let no one presume to ask any questions there, either about the book or anything else, in order that no cause to speak be given [to the devil] (Eph 4:27; 1 Tm 5:14), unless, perchance, the Superior wisheth to say a few words for edification.

Let the brother who is reader for the week take a little bread and wine before he beginneth to read, on account of Holy Communion, and lest it should be too hard for him to fast so long. Afterward, however, let him take his meal in the kitchen with the weekly servers and the waiters. The brethren, however, will not read or sing in order, but only those who edify their hearers.

CHAPTER XXXIX
Of the Quantity of Food

Making allowance for the infirmities of different persons, we believe that for the daily meal, both at the sixth and the ninth hour, two kinds of cooked food are sufficient at all meals; so that he who perchance cannot eat of one, may make his meal of the other. Let two kinds of cooked food, therefore, be sufficient for all the brethren. And if there be fruit or fresh vegetables, a third may be added. Let a pound of bread be sufficient for the day, whether there be only one meal or both dinner and supper. If they are to eat supper, let a third part of the pound be reserved by the Cellarer and be given at supper.

If, however, the work hath been especially hard, it is left to the discretion and power of the Abbot to add something, if he think fit, barring above all things every excess, that a monk be not overtaken by indigestion. For nothing is so contrary to Christians as excess, as our Lord saith: "See that your hearts be not overcharged with surfeiting" (Lk 21:34).

Let the same quantity of food, however, not be served out to young children but less than to older ones, observing measure in all things.

But let all except the very weak and the sick abstain altogether from eating the flesh of four-footed animals.

CHAPTER XL
Of the Quantity of Drink

"Every one hath his proper gift from God, one after this manner and another after that" (1 Cor 7:7). It is with some hesitation, therefore, that we determine the measure of nourishment for others. However, making allowance for the weakness of the infirm, we think one hemina of wine a day is sufficient for each one. But to whom God granteth the endurance of abstinence, let them know that they will have their special reward. If the circumstances of the place, or the work, or the summer's heat should require more, let that depend on the judgment of the Superior, who must above all things see to it, that excess or drunkenness do not creep in.

Although we read that wine is not at all proper for monks, yet, because monks in our times cannot be persuaded of this, let us agree to this, at least, that we do not drink to satiety, but sparingly; because "wine maketh even wise men fall off" (Sir 19:2). But where the poverty of the place will not permit the aforesaid measure to be had, but much less, or none at all, let those who live there bless God and murmur not. This we charge above all things, that they live without murmuring.

CHAPTER XLI
At What Times the Brethren Should Take Their Refection

From holy Easter till Pentecost let the brethren dine at the sixth hour and take supper in the evening. From Pentecost on, however, during the whole summer, if the monks have no work in the fields and the excess of the heat doth not interfere, let them fast on Wednesday and Friday until the ninth hour; but on the other days let them dine at the sixth hour. This sixth hour for dinner is to be continued, if they have work in the fields or the heat of the summer is great. Let the Abbot provide for this; and so let him manage and adapt everything that souls may be saved, and that what the brethren do, they may do without having a reasonable cause to murmur. From the ides of September until the beginning of Lent let them always dine at the ninth hour. During Lent, however, until Easter, let them dine in the evening. But let this evening hour be so arranged that they will not need lamp-light during their meal; but let everything be finished whilst it is still day. But at all times let the hour of meals, whether for dinner or for supper, be so arranged that everything is done by daylight.

CHAPTER XLII
That No One Speak after Complin

Monks should always be given to silence, especially, however, during the hours of the night. Therefore, on every day, whether of fast or of a mid-day meal, as soon as they have risen from their evening meal, let all sit together in one place, and let one read the Conferences or the Lives of the Fathers, or something else that will edify the hearers; not, however, the Heptateuch or the Books of the Kings, because it would not be wholesome for weak minds to hear this part of the Scripture at that hour; they should, however, be read at other times. But if it was a fast-day, then, when Vespers have been said, and after a short interval, let them next come together for the reading of the Conferences, as we have said; and when the four or five pages have been read, or as much as the hour will permit, and all have assembled in one place during the time of the reading, let him also come who was perchance engaged in work enjoined on him. All, therefore, having assembled in one place, let them say Complin, and after going out from Complin, let there be no more permission from that time on for anyone to say anything.

If, however, anyone is found to break this rule, let him undergo heavy punishment, unless the needs of guests should arise, or the Abbot should perhaps give a command to anyone. But let even this be done with the utmost gravity and moderation.

CHAPTER XLIII

Of Those Who Are Tardy in Coming to the Work of God or to Table

As soon as the signal for the time of the divine office is heard, let everyone, leaving whatever he hath in his hands, hasten with all speed, yet with gravity, that there may be no cause for levity. Therefore, let nothing be preferred to the Work of God. If at Matins anyone cometh after the *Gloria* of the 94th psalm, which on that account we wish to be much drawn out and said slowly, let him not stand in his place in the choir; but let him stand last of all, or in a place which the Abbot hath set apart for such careless ones, that he may be seen by him and by all, until, the Work of God being ended, he maketh satisfaction by public penance. The reason, however, why we think they should stand in the last place, or apart from the rest, is this, that seen by all they may amend for very shame. For if they stayed outside the oratory, there might be one who would go back to sleep, or anyhow would seat himself outside, indulge in vain gossip, and give a "chance to the devil" (Eph 4:27; 1 Tm 5:14). Let him go inside, therefore, that he may not lose the whole, and may amend for the future.

At the day hours, however, whoever doth not arrive for the Work of God after the verse and the *Gloria* of the first psalm, which is said after the verse, let him stand in the last place, according to the rule which we stated above; and let him not attempt to join the choir of the chanters until he hath made satisfaction, unless, perchance, the Abbot's permission hath given him leave to do so, with the understanding that he atone the fault afterwards.

If anyone doth not come to table before the verse, so that all may say the verse and pray together and sit down to table at the same time, let him be twice corrected for this, if he failed to come through his own fault and negligence. If he doth not amend after this, let him not be permitted to eat at the common table; but separated from the company of all, let him eat alone, his portion of wine being taken from him, until he hath made satisfaction and hath amended. In like manner let him suffer who is not present also at the verse which is said after the refection.

And let no one presume to take food or drink before or after the appointed time. But if anything should be offered to a brother by the Superior and he refuseth to accept it, and afterwards desireth what at first he refused or anything else, let him receive nothing at all, until he maketh due satisfaction.

CHAPTER XLIV

Of Those Who Are Excommunicated -- How They Make Satisfaction

Whoever is excommunicated for graver faults from the oratory and the table, let him, at the time that the Work of God is celebrated in the oratory, lie stretched, face down in silence before the door of the oratory at the feet of all who pass out. And let him do this until the Abbot judgeth that it is enough. When he then cometh at the Abbot's bidding, let him cast himself at the Abbot's feet, then at the feet of all, that they may pray for him. If then the Abbot ordereth it, let him be received back into the choir in the place which the Abbot shall direct; yet so that he doth not presume to intone a psalm or a lesson or anything else in the oratory, unless the Abbot again biddeth him to do so. Then, at all the Hours, when the Work of God is ended, let him cast himself on the ground in the place where he standeth, and thus let him make satisfaction, until the Abbot again biddeth him finally to cease from this penance.

But let those who are excommunicated for lighter faults from the table only make satisfaction in the oratory, as long as the Abbot commandeth, and let them perform this until he giveth his blessing and saith, "It is enough."

CHAPTER XLV
Of Those Who Commit a Fault in the Oratory

If anyone whilst he reciteth a psalm, a responsory, an antiphon, or a lesson, maketh a mistake, and doth not humble himself there before all by making satisfaction, let him undergo a greater punishment, because he would not correct by humility what he did amiss through negligence. But let children be beaten for such a fault.

CHAPTER XLVI
Of Those Who Fail in Any Other Matters

If anyone whilst engaged in any work, in the kitchen, in the cellar, in serving, in the bakery, in the garden, at any art or work in any place whatever, committeth a fault, or breaketh or loseth anything, or transgresseth in any way whatever, and he doth not forthwith come before the Abbot and the community, and of his own accord confess his offense and make satisfaction, and it becometh known through another, let him be subjected to a greater correction.

If, however, the cause of the offense is secret, let him disclose it to the Abbot alone, or to his spiritual Superiors, who know how to heal their own wounds, and not expose and make public those of others.

CHAPTER XLVII
Of Giving the Signal for the Time of the Work of God

Let it be the Abbot's care that the time for the Work of God be announced both by day and by night; either to announce it himself, or to entrust this charge to a careful brother that everything may be done at the proper time.

Let those who have been ordered, intone the psalms or the antiphons in their turn after the Abbot. No one, however, should presume to sing or read unless he is able so to perform this office that the hearers may be edified; and let it be done with humility, gravity, and reverence by him whom the Abbot hath ordered.

CHAPTER XLVIII
Of the Daily Work

Idleness is the enemy of the soul; and therefore the brethren ought to be employed in manual labor at certain times, at others, in devout reading. Hence, we believe that the time for each will be properly ordered by the following arrangement; namely, that from Easter till the calends of October, they go out in the morning from the first till about the fourth hour, to do the necessary work, but that from the fourth till about the sixth hour they devote to reading. After the sixth hour, however, when they have risen from table, let them rest in their beds in complete silence; or if, perhaps, anyone desireth to read for himself, let him so read that he doth not disturb others. Let None be said somewhat earlier, about the middle of the eighth hour; and then let them work again at what is necessary until Vespers.

If, however, the needs of the place, or poverty should require that they do the work of gathering the harvest themselves, let them not be downcast, for then are they monks in truth, if they live by the work of their hands, as did also our forefathers and the Apostles. However, on account of the faint-hearted let all things be done with moderation.

From the calends of October till the beginning
of Lent, let them apply themselves to reading
until the second hour complete. At the second
hour let Tierce be said, and then let all be
employed in the work which hath been assigned
to them till the ninth hour. When, however, the
first signal for the hour of None hath been
given, let each one leave off from work and be
ready when the second signal shall strike. But
after their repast let them devote themselves to
reading or the psalms.

During the Lenten season let them be employed
in reading from morning until the third hour,
and till the tenth hour let them do the work
which is imposed on them. During these days
of Lent let all received books from the library,
and let them read them through in order. These
books are to be given out at the beginning of
the Lenten season.

Above all, let one or two of the seniors be
appointed to go about the monastery during the
time that the brethren devote to reading and
take notice, lest perhaps a slothful brother be
found who giveth himself up to idleness or vain
talk, and doth not attend to his reading, and is
unprofitable, not only to himself, but disturbeth
also others. If such a one be found (which God
forbid), let him be punished once and again. If
he doth not amend, let him come under the

correction of the Rule in such a way that others may fear. And let not brother join brother at undue times.

On Sunday also let all devote themselves to reading, except those who are appointed to the various functions. But if anyone should be so careless and slothful that he will not or cannot meditate or read, let some work be given him to do, that he may not be idle.

Let such work or charge be given to the weak and the sickly brethren, that they are neither idle, nor so wearied with the strain of work that they are driven away. Their weakness must be taken into account by the Abbot.

CHAPTER XLIX
On the Keeping of Lent

The life of a monk ought always to be a Lenten observance. However, since such virtue is that of few, we advise that during these days of Lent he guard his life with all purity and at the same time wash away during these holy days all the shortcomings of other times. This will then be worthily done, if we restrain ourselves from all vices. Let us devote ourselves to tearful prayers, to reading and compunction of heart, and to abstinence.

During these days, therefore, let us add something to the usual amount of our service, special prayers, abstinence from food and drink, that each one offer to God "with the joy of the Holy Ghost" (1 Thes 1:6), of his own accord, something above his prescribed measure; namely, let him withdraw from his body somewhat of food, drink, sleep, speech, merriment, and with the gladness of spiritual desire await holy Easter.

Let each one, however, make known to his Abbot what he offereth and let it be done with his approval and blessing; because what is done without permission of the spiritual father will be imputed to presumption and vain glory, and not to merit. Therefore, let all be done with the approval of the Abbot.

CHAPTER L

Of Brethren Who Work a Long Distance from the Oratory or Are on a Journey

The brethren who are at work too far away, and cannot come to the oratory at the appointed time, and the Abbot hath assured himself that such is the case -- let them perform the Work of God in the fear of God and on bended knees where they are working. In like manner let those who are sent on a journey not permit the appointed hours to pass by; but let them say the office by themselves as best they can, and not neglect to fulfil the obligation of divine service.

CHAPTER LI
Of the Brethren Who Do Not Go Very Far Away

A brother who is sent out on any business and is expected to return to the monastery the same day, may not presume to eat outside, even though he be urgently requested to do so, unless, indeed, it is commanded him by his Abbot. If he act otherwise, let him be excommunicated.

CHAPTER LII
Of the Oratory of the Monastery

Let the oratory be what it is called, and let nothing else be done or stored there. When the Work of God is finished, let all go out with the deepest silence, and let reverence be shown to God; that a brother who perhaps desireth to pray especially by himself is not prevented by another's misconduct. But if perhaps another desireth to pray alone in private, let him enter with simplicity and pray, not with a loud voice, but with tears and fervor of heart. Therefore, let him who doth not say his prayers in this way, not be permitted to stay in the oratory after the

Work of God is finished, as we said, that
another may not be disturbed.

CHAPTER LIII
Of the Reception of Guests

Let all guests who arrive be received as Christ,
because He will say: "I was a stranger and you
took Me in" (Mt 25:35). And let due honor be
shown to all, especially to those "of the
household of the faith" (Gal 6:10) and to
wayfarers.

When, therefore, a guest is announced, let him
be met by the Superior and the brethren with
every mark of charity. And let them first pray
together, and then let them associate with one
another in peace. This kiss of peace should not
be given before a prayer hath first been said, on
account of satanic deception. In the greeting let
all humility be shown to the guests, whether
coming or going; with the head bowed down or
the whole body prostrate on the ground, let
Christ be adored in them as He is also received.

When the guests have been received, let them
be accompanied to prayer, and after that let the
Superior, or whom he shall bid, sit down with
them. Let the divine law be read to the guest
that he may be edified, after which let every
kindness be shown him. Let the fast be broken

by the Superior in deference to the guest, unless, perchance, it be a day of solemn fast, which cannot be broken. Let the brethren, however, keep the customary fast. Let the Abbot pour the water on the guest's hands, and let both the Abbot and the whole brotherhood wash the feet of all the guests. When they have been washed, let them say this verse: "We have received Thy mercy, O God, in the midst of Thy temple" (Ps 47[48]:10). Let the greatest care be taken, especially in the reception of the poor and travelers, because Christ is received more specially in them; whereas regard for the wealthy itself procureth them respect.

Let the kitchen of the Abbot and the guests be apart, that the brethren may not be disturbed by the guests who arrive at uncertain times and who are never wanting in the monastery. Let two brothers who are able to fulfil this office well go into the kitchen for a year. Let help be given them as they need it, that they may serve without murmuring; and when they have not enough to do, let them go out again for work where it is commanded them. Let this course be followed, not only in this office, but in all the offices of the monastery -- that whenever the brethren need help, it be given them, and that when they have nothing to do, they again obey orders. Moreover, let also a God-fearing brother have assigned to him the apartment of the guests, where there should be sufficient number of beds made up; and let the house of God be wisely managed by the wise.

On no account let anyone who is not ordered to do so, associate or speak with guests; but if he meet or see them, having saluted them humbly, as we have said, and asked a blessing, let him pass on saying that he is not allowed to speak with a guest.

CHAPTER LIV
Whether a Monk Should Receive Letters or Anything Else

Let it not be allowed at all for a monk to give or to receive letters, tokens, or gifts of any kind, either from parents or any other person, nor from each other, without the permission of the Abbot. But even if anything is sent him by his parents, let him not presume to accept it before it hath been make known to the Abbot. And if he order it to be accepted, let it be in the Abbot's power to give it to whom he pleaseth. And let not the brother to whom perchance it was sent, become sad, that "no chance be given to the devil" (Eph 4:27; 1 Tm 5:14). But whosoever shall presume to act otherwise, let him fall under the discipline of the Rule.

CHAPTER LV

Of the Clothing and the Footgear of the Brethren

Let clothing be given to the brethren according to the circumstances of the place and the nature of the climate in which they live, because in cold regions more in needed, while in warm regions less. This consideration, therefore, resteth with the Abbot. We believe, however, that for a temperate climate a cowl and a tunic for each monk are sufficient, -- a woolen cowl for winter and a thin or worn one for summer, and a scapular for work, and stockings and shoes as covering for the feet. Let the monks not worry about the color or the texture of all these things, but let them be such as can be bought more cheaply. Let the Abbot, however, look to the size, that these garments are not too small, but fitted for those who are to wear them.

Let those who receive new clothes always return the old ones, to be put away in the wardrobe for the poor. For it is sufficient for a monk to have two tunics and two cowls, for wearing at night and for washing. Hence, what is over and above is superfluous and must be taken away. So, too, let them return stockings and whatever is old, when they receive anything new. Let those who are sent out on a journey receive trousers from the wardrobe, which, on their return, they will replace there, washed. The cowls and the tunics should also be a little better than the ones they usually wear, which they received from the wardrobe when they set out on a journey, and give back when they return.

For their bedding, let a straw mattress, a blanket, a coverlet, and a pillow be sufficient. These beds must, however, be frequently examined by the Abbot, to prevent personal goods from being found. And if anything should be found with anyone that he did not receive from the Abbot, let him fall under the severest discipline. And that this vice of private ownership may be cut off by the root, let everything necessary be given by the Abbot; namely, cowl, tunic, stockings, shoes, girdle, knife, pen, needle, towel, writing tablet; that all pretence of want may be removed. In this connection, however, let the following sentence from the Acts of the Apostles always be kept in mind by the Abbot: "And distribution was made to every man according as he had need" (Acts 4:35). In this manner, therefore, let the Abbot also have regard for the infirmities of the needy, not for the bad will of the envious. Yet in all his decisions, let the Abbot think of God's retribution.

CHAPTER LVI
Of the Abbot's Table

Let the Abbot's table always be with the guests and travelers. When, however, there are no guests, let it be in his power to invite any of the brethren he desireth. Let him provide, however, that one or two of the seniors always remain with the brethren for the sake of discipline.

CHAPTER LVII
Of the Artists of the Monastery

If there be skilled workmen in the monastery, let them work at their art in all humility, if the Abbot giveth his permission. But if anyone of them should grow proud by reason of his art, in that he seemeth to confer a benefit on the monastery, let him be removed from that work and not return to it, unless after he hath humbled himself, the Abbot again ordereth him to do so. But if any of the work of the artists is to be sold, let them, through whose hands the transaction must pass, see to it, that they do not presume to practice any fraud on the monastery. Let them always be mindful of Ananias and Saphira, lest, perhaps, the death which these suffered in the body (cf Acts 5:1-11), they and all who practice any fraud in things belonging to the monastery suffer in the soul. On the other hand, as regards the prices of these things, let not the vice of avarice creep in, but let it always be given a little cheaper than it can be given by seculars, **That God May Be Glorified in All Things** (1 Pt 4:11).

CHAPTER LVIII
Of the Manner of Admitting Brethren

Let easy admission not be given to one who newly cometh to change his life; but, as the Apostle saith, "Try the spirits, whether they be of God" (1 Jn 4:1). If, therefore, the newcomer keepeth on knocking, and after four or five days it is seen that he patiently beareth the harsh treatment offered him and the difficulty of admission, and that he persevereth in his request, let admission be granted him, and let him live for a few days in the apartment of the guests.

But afterward let him live in the apartment of novices, and there let him meditate, eat, and sleep. Let a senior also be appointed for him, who is qualified to win souls, who will observe him with great care and see whether he really seeketh God, whether he is eager for the Work of God, obedience and humiliations. Let him be shown all the hard and rugged things through which we pass on to God.

If he promiseth to remain steadfast, let this Rule be read to him in order after the lapse of two months, and let it be said to him: Behold the law under which thou desirest to combat. If thou canst keep it, enter; if, however, thou canst not, depart freely. If he still persevereth, then let him be taken back to the aforesaid apartment of the novices, and let him be tried again in all patience. And after the lapse of six months let the Rule be read over to him, that he may know for what purpose he entereth. And if he still remaineth firm, let the same Rule be read to him again after four months. And if, after having weighed the matter with himself he promiseth to keep everything, and to do everything that is commanded him, then let him be received into the community, knowing that he is now placed under the law of the Rule, and that from that day forward it is no longer permitted to him to wrest his neck from under the yoke of the Rule, which after so long a deliberation he was at liberty either to refuse or to accept.

Let him who is received promise in the oratory, in the presence of all, before God and His saints, stability, the conversion of morals, and obedience, in order that, if he should ever do otherwise, he may know that he will be condemned by God "Whom he mocketh." Let him make a written statement of his promise in the name of the saints whose relics are there, and of the Abbot there present. Let him write this document with his own hand; or at least, if he doth not know how to write, let another write it at his request, and let the novice make his mark, and with his own hand place it on the altar. When he hath placed it there, let the novice next begin the verse: "Uphold me, O Lord, according to Thy word and I shall live; and let me not be confounded in my expectations" (Ps 118[119]:116). Then let all the brotherhood repeat this verse three times, adding the *Gloria Patri.*

The let that novice brother cast himself down at the feet of all, that they may pray for him; and from that day let him be counted in the brotherhood. If he hath any property, let him first either dispose of it to the poor or bestow it on the monastery by a formal donation, reserving nothing for himself as indeed he should know that from that day onward he will no longer have power even over his own body.

Let him, therefore, be divested at once in the oratory of the garments with which he is clothed, and be vested in the garb of the monastery. But let the clothes of which he was divested by laid by in the wardrobe to be preserved, that, if on the devil's suasion he should ever consent to leave the monastery (which God forbid) he be then stripped of his monastic habit and cast out. But let him not receive the document of his profession which the Abbot took from the altar, but let it be preserved in the monastery.

CHAPTER LIX
Of the Children of the Noble and of the Poor Who Are Offered

If it happen that a nobleman offereth his son to God in the monastery and the boy is of tender age, let his parents execute the written promise which we have mentioned above; and with the oblation let them wrap that document and the boy's hand in the altar cloth and thus offer him.

As to their property, let them bind themselves under oath in the same document that they will never give him anything themselves nor through any other person, nor in any way whatever, nor leave a chance for his owning anything; or else, if they refuse to do this and want to make an offering to the monastery as an alms for their own benefit, let them make a donation to the monastery of whatever goods they wish to give, reserving to themselves the income of it, if they so desire. And let everything be so barred that the boy remain in no uncertainty, which might deceive and ruin him (which God forbid) -- a pass we have learned by experience.

Let those who are poor act in like manner. But as to those who have nothing at all, let them simply make the declaration, and with the oblation offer their son in the presence of witnesses.

CHAPTER LX

Of Priests Who May Wish to Live in the Monastery

If a priest asketh to be received into the monastery, let consent not be granted too readily; still, if he urgently persisteth in his request, let him know that he must keep the whole discipline of the Rule, and that nothing will be relaxed in his favor, that it may be as it is written: "Friend, whereunto art thou come" (Mt 26:25)?

It may be granted him, however, to stand next after the Abbot, and to give the blessing, or to celebrate Mass, but only if the Abbot ordereth him to do so; but if he doth not bid him, let him not presume to do anything under whatever consideration, knowing that he is under the discipline of the Rule, and let him rather give examples of humility to all. But if there is a question of an appointment in the monastery, or any other matter, let him be ranked by the time of his entry into the monastery, and not by the place granted him in consideration of the priesthood.

But if a cleric, moved by the same desire, wisheth to join the monastery, let him too have a middle place, provided he promiseth to keep the Rule and personal stability.

CHAPTER LXI
How Stranger Monks Are to Be Received

If a monk who is a stranger, arriveth from a distant place and desireth to live in the monastery as a guest, and is satisfied with the customs he findeth there, and doth not trouble the monastery with superfluous wants, but is satisfied with what he findeth, let him be received for as long a time as he desireth. Still, if he should reasonably, with humility and charity, censure or point out anything, let the Abbot consider discreetly whether the Lord did not perhaps send him for that very purpose. If later on he desireth to declare his stability let his wish not be denied, and especially since his life could be known during his stay as a guest.

But if during the time that he was a guest he was found to be troublesome and disorderly, he must not only not associate with the monastic body but should even be politely requested to leave, that others may not be infected by his evil life. But if he hath not been such as deserveth to be cast forth, he should not only be admitted to join the brotherhood, if he apply, but he should even be urged to remain, that others may be taught by his example, because we serve one Lord and fight under one King everywhere. If the Abbot recognize him to be such a one he may also place him in a somewhat higher rank.

The Abbot may, however, place not only a monk, but also those of the aforesaid grades of priests and clerics, in a higher place than that of their entry, if he seeth their lives to be such as to deserve it. But let the Abbot take care never to admit a monk of any other known monastery to residence, without the consent of his Abbot or commendatory letters, because it is written: "What thou wilt not have done to thyself, do not to another" (Tb 4:16).

CHAPTER LXII
Of the Priests of the Monastery

If the Abbot desireth to have a priest or a deacon ordained, let him select from among his monks one who is worthy to discharge the priestly office.

But let the one who hath been ordained be on his guard against arrogance and pride, and let him not attempt to do anything but what is commanded him by the Abbot, knowing that he is now all the more subject to the discipline of the Rule; and in consequence of the priesthood let him not forget the obedience and discipline of the Rule, but advance more and more in godliness.

Let him, however, always keep the place which he had when he entered the monastery, except when he is engaged in sacred functions, unless the choice of the community and the wish of the Abbot have promoted him in acknowledgment of the merit of his life. Let him know, however, that he must observe the Rule prescribed by the Deans and the Superiors.

If he should otherwise, let him be judged, not as a priest, but as a rebel; and if after frequent warnings he doth not amend, and his guilt is clearly shown, let him be cast forth from the monastery, provided his obstinacy is such that he will neither submit nor obey the Rule.

CHAPTER LXIII
Of the Order in the Monastery

Let all keep their order in the monastery in such wise, that the time of their conversion and the merit of their life distinguish it, or as the Abbot hath directed. Let the Abbot not disorder the flock committed to him, nor by an arbitrary use of his power dispose of anything unjustly; but let him always bear in mind that he will have to give an account to God of all his judgments and works. Hence in the order that he hath established, or that the brethren had, let them approach for the kiss of peace, for Communion, intone the psalms, and stand in choir.

And in no place whatever let age determine the order or be a disadvantage; because Samuel and Daniel when mere boys judged the priests (cf 1 Sam 3; Dan 13:44-62). Excepting those, therefore, whom, as we have said, the Abbot from higher motives hath advanced, or, for certain reasons, hath lowered, let all the rest take their place as they are converted: thus, for instance, let him who came into the monastery at the second hour of the day, know that he is younger than he who came at the first hour, whatever his age or dignity may be.

Children are to be kept under discipline at all times and by everyone. Therefore, let the younger honor their elders, and the older love the younger.

In naming each other let no one be allowed to address another by his simple name; but let the older style the younger brethren, brothers; let the younger, however, call their elders, fathers, by which is implied the reverence due to a father. But because the Abbot is believed to hold the place of Christ, let him be styled Lord and Abbot, not only by assumption on his part, but out of love and reverence for Christ. Let him think of this and so show himself, that he be worthy of such an honor. Wherever, then, the brethren meet each other, let the younger ask the blessing from the older; and when the older passeth by, let the younger rise and give him place to sit; and let the younger not presume to sit down with him unless his elder biddeth him to do so, that it may be done as it is written: "In honor preventing one another" (Rom 12:10).

Let children and boys take their places in the oratory and at table with all due discipline; outdoors, however, or wherever they may be, let them be under custody and discipline until they reach the age of understanding.

CHAPTER LXIV
Of the Election of the Abbot

In the election of an Abbot let this always be observed as a rule, that he be placed in the position whom the whole community with one consent, in the fear of God, or even a small part, with sounder judgment, shall elect. But let him who is to be elected be chosen for the merit of his life and the wisdom of his doctrine, though he be the last in the community.

But even if the whole community should by mutual consent elect a man who agreeth to connive at their evil ways (which God forbid) and these irregularities in some come to the knowledge of the Bishop to whose diocese the place belongeth, or to neighboring Abbots, or Christian people, let them not permit the intrigue of the wicked to succeed, but let them appoint a worthy steward over the house of God, knowing that they shall receive a bountiful reward for this action, if they do it with a pure intention and godly zeal; whereas, on the other hand, they commit a sin if they neglect it.

But when the Abbot hath been elected let him bear in mind how great a burden he hath taken upon himself, and to whom he must give an account of his stewardship (cf Lk 16:2); and let him be convinced that it becometh him better to serve than to rule. He must, therefore, be versed in the divine law, that he may know whence "to bring forth new things and old" (Mt 13:52). Let him be chaste, sober, and merciful, and let him always exalt "mercy above judgment" (Jas 2:13), that he also may obtain mercy.

Let him hate vice, but love the brethren. And even in his corrections, let him act with prudence and not go to extremes, lest, while he aimeth to remove the rust too thoroughly, the vessel be broken. Let him always keep his own frailty in mind, and remember that "the bruised reed must not be broken" (Is 42:3). In this we are not saying that he should allow evils to take root, but that he cut them off with prudence and charity, as he shall see it is best for each one, as we have already said; and let him aim to be loved rather than feared.

Let him not be fussy or over-anxious, exacting, or headstrong; let him not be jealous or suspicious, because he will never have rest. In all his commands, whether they refer to things spiritual or temporal, let him be cautious and considerate. Let him be discerning and temperate in the tasks which he enjoineth, recalling the discretion of holy Jacob who saith: "If I should cause my flocks to be overdriven, they would all die in one day" (Gen 33:13). Keeping in view these and other dictates of discretion, the mother of virtues, let him so temper everything that the strong may still have something to desire and the weak may not draw back. Above all, let him take heed that he keep this Rule in all its detail; that when he hath served well he may hear from the Lord what the good servant heard who gave his fellow-servants bread in season: "Amen, I say to you," He saith, "he shall set him over all his goods" (Mt 24:47).

CHAPTER LXV
Of the Prior of the Monastery

It often happeneth indeed, that grave scandals arise in monasteries out of the appointment of the Prior; since there are some who, puffed up with the wicked spirit of pride and thinking themselves to be second Abbots, set up a despotic rule, foster scandals, and excite quarrels in the community, and especially in those places where also the Prior is appointed by the same Bishop or the same Abbots who appointeth his Abbot. How foolish this is can easily be seen; because, from the very beginning of his appointment, matter for pride is furnished him, when his thoughts suggest to him that now he is exempt from the authority of the Abbot, because "thou too hast been appointed by those by whom the Abbot was appointed." From this source arise envy, discord, slander, quarrels, jealousy, and disorders. While the Abbot and the Prior are thus at variance with each other, it must follow that their souls are endangered by this discord and that those who are under them, as long as they humor the parties, go to ruin. The fault of this evil resteth on the heads of those who were the authors of such disorders.

We foresee, therefore, that for the preservation of peace and charity it is best that the government of the monastery should depend on the will of the Abbot; and if it can be done, let the affairs of the monastery (as we have explained before) be attended to by deans, as the Abbot shall dispose; so that, the same office being shared by many, no one may become proud.

If, however, the place require it, or the brotherhood reasonably and with humility make the request, and the Abbot shall deem it advisable, let the Abbot himself appoint as Prior whomever, with the advice of God-fearing brethren, he shall select. But let the Prior reverently do what his Abbot hath enjoined on him, doing nothing against the will or the direction of the Abbot; for the higher he is placed above others, the more careful should he be to obey the precepts of the Rule.

If the Prior be found disorderly or blinded by vainglory, or hath been proved to be a contemner of the Holy Rule, let him be admonished up to the fourth time; if he doth not amend, let the correction of the regular discipline be applied to him. But if he doth not amend even then, let him be deposed from the office of priorship, and another who is worthy be appointed in his stead. But if even afterward he be not quiet and submissive in the brotherhood, let him also be expelled from the monastery. Still, let the Abbot reflect that he must give an account to God for all his judgments, lest perhaps envy or jealousy should sear his conscience.

CHAPTER LXVI
Of the Porter of the Monastery

Let a wise old man be placed at the door of the monastery, one who knoweth how to take and give an answer, and whose mature age doth not permit him to stray about.

The porter should have a cell near the door, that they who come may always find one present from whom they may obtain an answer. As soon as anyone knocketh or a poor person calleth, let him answer, "Thanks be to God," or invoke a blessing, and with the meekness of the fear of God let him return an answer speedily in the fervor of charity. If the porter hath need of assistance, let him have a younger brother.

If it can be done, the monastery should be so situated that all the necessaries, such as water, the mill, the garden, are enclosed, and the various arts may be plied inside of the monastery, so that there may be no need for the monks to go about outside, because it is not good for their souls. But we desire that this Rule be read quite often in the community, that none of the brethren may excuse himself of ignorance.

CHAPTER LXVII

Of the Brethren Who Are Sent on a Journey

Let the brethren who are to be sent on a journey recommend themselves to the prayers of all the brotherhood and of the Abbot. And after the last prayer at the Work of God, let a commemoration always be made for the absent brethren.

On the day that the brethren return from the journey, let them lie prostrate on the floor of the oratory at all the Canonical Hours, when the Work of God is finished, and ask the prayers of all on account of failings, for fear that the sight of evil or the sound of frivolous speech should have surprised them on the way.

And let no one presume to relate to another what he hath seen or heard outside of the monastery, because it is most hurtful. But if anyone presume to do so, let him undergo the penalty of the Rule. In like manner let him be punished who shall presume to go beyond the enclosure of the monastery, or anywhere else, or to do anything, however little, without the order of the Abbot.

CHAPTER LXVIII
If a Brother Is Commanded to Do Impossible Things

If, perchance, any difficult or impossible tasks be enjoined on a brother, let him nevertheless receive the order of him who commandeth with all meekness and obedience. If, however, he see that the gravity of the task is altogether beyond his strength, let him quietly and seasonably submit the reasons for his inability to his Superior, without pride, protest, or dissent. If, however, after his explanation the Superior still insisteth on his command, let the younger be convinced that so it is good for him; and let him obey from love, relying on the help of God.

CHAPTER LXIX
That in the Monastery No One Presume to Defend Another

Care must be taken that on no occasion one monk try to defend another in the monastery, or to take his part, even though they be closely related by ties of blood. Let it not be attempted by the monks in any way; because such conduct may give rise to very grave scandal. If anyone overstep this rule, let him be severely punished.

CHAPTER LXX
That No One Presume to Strike Another

Let every occasion for presumption be avoided in the monastery. We decree that no one be permitted to excommunicate or to strike any one of his brethren, unless the Abbot hath given him the authority. But let those who transgress be taken to task in the presence of all, that the others may fear (cf 1 Tm 5:20).

Let all, however, exercise diligent and watchful care over the discipline of children, until the age of fifteen; but even that, within due limits and with discretion. For if anyone should presume to chastise those of more advanced years, without the command of the Abbot, or should be unduly provoked with children, let him be subject the discipline of the Rule; because it is written: "What thou dost not wish to be done to thee, do not thou to another" (Tb 4:16).

CHAPTER LXXI

That the Brethren Be Obedient to One Another

The brethren must render the service of obedience not only to the Abbot, but they must thus also obey one another, knowing that they shall go to God by this path of obedience. Hence, granted the command of the Abbot and of the Superiors who are appointed by him (to which we do not permit private commands to be preferred), in other respects let the younger brethren obey their elders with all charity and zeal. But if anyone is found to be obstinate, let him be punished.

And if a brother be punished in any way by the Abbot or by any of his Superiors for even a slight reason or if he perceive that the temper of any of his Superiors is but slightly ruffled or excited against him in the least, let him without delay cast himself down on the ground at his feet making satisfaction, until the agitation is quieted by a blessing. If anyone scorn to do this, either let him undergo corporal punishment, or, if he be obstinate, let him be expelled from the monastery.

CHAPTER LXXII
Of the Virtuous Zeal Which the Monks Ought to Have

As there is a harsh and evil zeal which separateth from God and leadeth to hell, so there is a virtuous zeal which separateth from vice and leadeth to God and life everlasting.

Let the monks, therefore, practice this zeal with most ardent love; namely, that in honor they forerun one another (cf Rom 12:10). Let them bear their infirmities, whether of body or mind, with the utmost patience; let them vie with one another in obedience. Let no one follow what he thinketh useful to himself, but rather to another. Let them practice fraternal charity with a chaste love.

Let them fear God and love their Abbot with sincere and humble affection; let them prefer nothing whatever to Christ, and my He lead us all together to life everlasting.

CHAPTER LXXIII
Of This, that Not the Whole Observance of Righteousness Is Laid Down in this Rule

Now, we have written this Rule that, observing it in monasteries, we may show that we have acquired at least some moral righteousness, or a beginning of the monastic life.

On the other hand, he that hasteneth on to the perfection of the religious life, hath at hand the teachings of the holy Fathers, the observance of which leadeth a man to the height of perfection. For what page or what utterance of the divinely inspired books of the Old and the New Testament is not a most exact rule of human life? Or, what book of the holy Catholic Fathers doth not loudly proclaim how we may go straight to our Creator? So, too, the collations of the Fathers, and their institutes and lives, and the rule of our holy Father, Basil -- what are they but the monuments of the virtues of exemplary and obedient monks? But for us slothful, disedifying, and negligent monks they are a source for shame and confusion.

Thou, therefore, who hastenest to the heavenly home, with the help of Christ fulfil this least rule written for a beginning; and then thou shalt with God's help attain at last to the greater heights of knowledge and virtue which we have mentioned above.

U. I. O. G. D.

Regula Sanctissimi Patris Benedicti

Regula Sanctissimi Patris Benedicti

Incipit prologus

Obsculta, o fili, præcepta magistri, et inclina aurem cordis tui et admonitionem pii patris libenter excipe et efficaciter conple, ut ad eum per oboedientiæ laborem redeas, a quo per inoboedientiæ desidiam recesseras. Ad te ergo nunc mihi sermo dirigitur, quisquis abrenuntians propriis voluntatibus, Domino Christo vero Regi militaturus oboedientiæ fortissima atque præclara arma sumis. In primis, ut quidquid agendum inchoas bonum, ab eo perfici instantissima oratione deposcas, ut qui nos iam in filiorum dignatus est numero conputare, non debet aliquando de malis actibus nostris contristari. Ita enim ei omni tempore de bonis suis in nobis parendum est ut non solum iratus pater suos non aliquando filios exheredet, sed nec ut metuendus dominus inritatus a malis nostris, ut nequissimos servos perpetuam tradat ad poenam qui eum sequi noluerint ad gloriam.

Exurgamus ergo tandem aliquando excitante nos Scriptura ac dicente: *Hora est iam nos de somno surgere*, et apertis oculis nostris ad deificum lumen adtonitis auribus audiamus divina cotidie clamans quid nos admonet vox dicens: *Hodie si vocem eius audieritis, nolite obdurare corda vestra.* Et iterum: *Qui habet aures audiendi audiat, quid Spiritus dicat ecclesiis.* Et quid dicit? *Venite, filii, audite me; timorem Dei docebo vos. Currite dum lumen vitæ habetis, ne tenebræ mortis vos conprehendant.*

Et quærens Dominus in multitudine populi cui hæc clamat operarium suum iterum dicit: *Quis est homo qui vult vitam et cupit videre dies bonos?* Quod si tu audiens respondeas: Ego, dicit tibi Deus: *Si vis habere veram et perpetuam vitam, prohibe linguam tuam a malo et labia tua ne loquantur dolum; deverte a malo et fac bonum, inquire pacem et sequere eam. Et cum hæc feceritis, oculi mei super vos et aures meas ad preces vestras, et antequam me invocetis, dicam vobis: Ecce adsum.* Quid dulcius ab hac voce Domini invitantis nos, fratres carissimi? Ecce pietate sua demonstrat nobis Dominus viam vitæ.

Succinctis ergo fide vel observantia bonorum actuum lumbis nostris, per ducatum Evangelii pergamus itinera eius, ut mereamur eum qui nos vocavit in regnum suum videre. In cujus regni tabernaculo si volumus habitare, nisi illuc bonis actibus curritur, minime pervenitur. Sed interrogemus cum Propheta Dominum dicentes ei: *Domine, quis habitabit in tabernaculo tuo, aut quis requiescet in monte sancto tuo?* Post hanc interrogationem, fratres, audiamus Dominum respondentem et ostendentem nobis viam ipsius tabernaculi, dicens: *Qui ingreditur sine macula et operatur iustitiam; qui loquitur veritatem in corde suo, qui non egit dolum in lingua sua; qui non fecit proximo suo malum, qui obprobrium non accepit adversus proximum suum*; qui malignum diabulum aliqua suadentem sibi cum ipsa suasione sua a conspectibus cordis sui respuens deduxit ad nihilum, et parvulos cogitatos eius tenuit et adlisit ad Christum; qui timentes Dominum de bona observantia sua non se reddunt elatos, sed ipsa in se bona non a se posse, sed a Domino fieri existimantes, operantem in se Dominum magnificant, illud cum Propheta dicentes: *Non nobis, Domine, non nobis, sed nomini tuo da gloriam*; sicut nec Paulus Apostolus de prædicatione sua sibi aliquid inputavit dicens: *Gloria Dei sum id quod sum*; et iterum ipse dicit: *Qui gloriatur, in Domino glorietur.*

Unde et Dominus in Evangelio ait: *Qui audit verba mea hæc et facit ea, similabo eum viro sapienti qui ædificavit domum suam super petram; venerunt flumina, flaverunt venti, et inpegerunt in domum illam, et non cecidit, quia fundata erat super petram.* Hæc conplens Dominus expectat nos cotidie his suis sanctis monitis factis nos respondere debere. Ideo nobis propter emendationem malorum huius vitæ dies ad indutias relaxantur, dicente Apostolo: *An nescis quia patientia Dei ad pænitentiam te adducit?* Nam pius Dominus dicit: *Nolo mortem peccatoris, sed convertatur et vivat.*

Cum ergo interrogassemus Dominum, fratres, de habitatore tabernaculi eius, audivimus habitandi præceptum; sed si conpleamus habitatoris officium, erimus heredes regni cælorum. Ergo præparanda sunt corda nostra et corpora sanctæ præceptorum oboedientiæ militanda, et quod minus habet in nos natura possibile, rogemus Dominum, ut gratiæ suæ iubeat nobis adiutorium ministrare. Et si, fugientes gehennæ poenas, ad vitam volumus pervenire perpetuam, dum adhuc vacat et in hoc corpore sumus et hæc omnia per hanc lucis vitam vacat implere, currendum et agendum est modo quod in perpetuo nobis expediat.

Constituenda est ergo nobis dominici scola servitii. In qua institutione nihil asperum, nihil grave nos constituturos speramus; sed et si quid paululum restrictius, dictante æquitatis ratione, propter emendationem vitiorum vel conservationem caritatis processerit, non ilico pavore perterritus refugias viam salutis, quæ non est nisi angusto initio incipienda. Processu vero conversationis et fidei, dilatato corde inenarrabili dilectionis dulcedine curritur via mandatorum Dei, ut ab ipsius numquam magisterio discedentes, in eius doctrinam usque ad mortem in monasterio perseverantes passionibus Christi per patientiam participemur, ut et regno eius mereamur esse consortes. Amen.

Caput 1: De generibus monachorum

Monachorum quattuor esse genera, manifestum est. Primum coenobitarum, hoc est

monasteriale, militans sub regula vel abbate.
Deinde secundum genus est anachoritarum id
est heremitarum, horum qui non conversationis
fervore novicio, sed monasterii probatione
diuturna, qui didicerunt contra diabulum
multorum solacio iam docti pugnare, et bene
extructi fraterna ex acie ad singularem pugnam
heremi, securi iam sine consolatione alterius,
sola manu vel brachio contra vitia carnis vel
cogitationum, Deo auxiliante, pugnare
sufficiunt.

Tertium vero monachorum teterrimum genus
est sarabaitarum, qui nulla regula adprobati,
experienta magistra, sicut aurum fornacis, sed in
plumbi natura molliti, adhuc operibus servantes
sæculo fidem, mentiri Deo per tonsuram
noscuntur. Qui bini aut terni aut certe singuli
sine pastore, non dominicis sed suis inclusi
ovilibus, pro lege eis est desideriorum voluptas,
cum quidquid putaverint vel elegerint, hoc
dicunt sanctum, et quod noluerint, hoc putant
non licere. Quartum vero genus est
monachorum quod nominatur girovagum, qui
tota vita sua per diversas provincias ternis aut

quaternis diebus per diversorum cellas
hospitantur, semper vagi et numquam stabiles,
et propriis voluntatibus et guilæ inlecebris
servientes, et per omnia deteriores sarabaitis. De
quorum omnium horum miserrima
conversatione melius est silere quam loqui. His
ergo omissis, ad coenobitarum fortissimum
genus disponendum, adiuvante Domino,
veniamus.

Caput 2: Qualis debeat esse abbas

Abbas qui præesse dignus est monasterio
semper meminere debet quod dicitur et nomen
maioris factis implere. Christi enim agere vices
in monasterio creditur, quando ipsius vocatur
pronomine, dicente apostolo: *Accepistis spiritum
adoptionis filiorum, in quo clamamus: Abba, Pater.*
Ideoque abbas nihil extra præceptum Domini
quod sit debet aut docere aut constituere vel
iubere, sed iussio eius vel doctrina fermentum
divinæ iustitiæ in discipulorum mentibus
conspargatur, memor semper abbas quia
doctrinæ suæ vel discipulorum oboedientiæ,
utrarumque rerum, in tremendo iudicio Dei
facienda erit discussio. Sciatque abbas culpæ

pastotis incumbere quidquid in ovibus paterfamilias utilitatis minus potuerit invenire. Tantumdem iterum erit ut, si inquieto vel inoboedienti gregi pastoris fuerit omnis diligentia adtributa et morbidis earum actibus universa fuerit cura exhibita, pastor eorum in iudicio Domini absolutus dicat cum Propheta Domino: *Iustitiam tuam non abscondi in corde meo, veritatem tuam et salutare tuum dixi; ipsi autem contemnentes spreverunt me*, et tunc demum inoboetientibus cursæ suæ ovibus poena sit eis prævalens ipsa mors.

Ergo, cum aliquis suscipit nomen abbatis, duplici debet doctrina suis præesse discipulis, id est omnia bona et sancta factis amplius quam verbis ostendat, ut capacibus discipulis mandata Domini verbis proponere, duris corde vero et simplicioribus factis suis divina præcepta monstrare. Omnia vero quæ discipulis docuerit esse contraria, in suis factis indicet non agenda, *ne aliis prædicans ipse reprobus inveniatur*, ne quando illi *dicat Deus precanti: quare tu enarras iustitias meas et adsumis testamentum meum per os tuum? tu vero odisti disciplinam et proiecisti sermones meos post te*, et:qui *in fratris tui oculo festucam videbas, in tuo trabem non vidisti.*

Non ab eo persona in monasterio discernatur. Non unus plus ametur quam alius, nisi quem in bonis actibus aut oboedientia invenerit meliorem. Non convertenti ex servitio præponatur ingenuus, nisi alia rationabilis causa existat. Quod si ita, iustitia dictante, abbati visum fuerit, et de cuiuslibet ordine id faciet; sin alias, propria teneant loca, quia: *Sive servus sive liber, omnes in Christo unum sumus* et sub uno Domino æqualem servitutis militiam baiulamus, quia: *Non est apud Deum personarum acceptio.* Solummodo in hac parte apud ipsum discernimur, si meliores ab aliis in operibus bonis et humiles inveniamur. Ergo æqualis sit ab eo omnibus caritas, una præ beatur in omnibus secundum merita disciplina.

In doctrina sua namque abbas apostolicam debet illam semper formam servare in qua dicit: *Argue, obsecra, increpa,* id est, miscens temporibus tempora, terroribus blandimenta, dirum magistri, pium patris ostendat affectum, id est indisciplinatos et inquietos debet durius arguere,

oboedientes autem et mites et patientes, ut in
melius proficiant obsecrare, neglegentes et
contemnentes ut increpat et corripiat
admonemus. Neque dissimulet peccata
delinquentiump; sed ut, mox ut coeperint oriri,
radicitus ea ut prævalet amputet, memor periculi
Heli sacerdotis de Silo. Et honestiores quidem
atque intellegibiles animos prima vel secunda
admonitione verbis corripiat, inprobos autem et
duros ac superbos vel inoboedientes verberum
vel corporis castigatio in ipso initio peccati
coerceat, sciens scriptum: *Stultus verbis non
corrigitur*, et iterum: *Percute filium tuum virga et
liberabis animam eius a morte.*

Meminere debet semper abbas quod est,
meminere quod dicitur, et scire quia cui plus
committitur, plus ab eo exigitur. Sciatque quam
difficilem et arduam rem suscipit, regere animas
et multorum servire moribus, et alium quidem
blandimentis, alium vero increpationibus, alium
suasionibus; et secundum unuscuiusque
qualitatem vel intellegentiam, ita se omnibus
conformet et aptet ut non solum detrimenta

gregis sibi commissi non patiatur, verum in
augmentatione boni gregis gaudeat.

Ante omnia, ne dissimulans aut parvipendens
salutem animarum sibi commissarum, ne plus
gerat sollicitudinem de rebus transitoriis et
terrenis atque caducis, sed semper cogitet quia
animas suscepit regendas, de quibus et rationem
redditurus est. Et ne causetur de minori forte
substantia , meminerit scriptum: *Primum quærite
regnum Dei et iustitiam eius, et hæc omnia adicientur
vobis*, et iterum: *Nihil deest timentibus eum.* Sciatque
quia qui suscipit animas regendas paret se ad
rationem reddendam. Et quantum sub cura sua
fratrum se habere scierit numerum, agnoscat
pro certo quia in die iudicii ipsarum omnium
animarum est redditurus Domino rationem, sine
dubio addita et suæ animæ. Et ita, timens
semper futuram discussionem pastoris de
creditis ovibus, cum de aliis ratiociniis cavet,
redditur de suis sollicitus, et cum de
monitionibus suis emendationem aliis
subministrat, ipse efficitur a vitiis emendatus.

Caput 3: De adhibendis ad consilium fratribus

Quotiens aliqua præcipua sunt in monasterio, convocet abbas omnem congregationem et dicat ipse unde agitur. Et audiens consilium fratrum tractet apud se et quod utilius iudicaverit faciat. Ideo autem omnes ad consilium vocari diximus, quia sæpe iuniori Dominus revelat quod melius est. Sic autem dent fratres consilium cum omni humilitatis subiectione, et non præsumant procaciter defendere quod eis visum fuerit; et magis in abbatis pendat arbitrio, ut quod salubrius esse iudicaverit, ei cuncti oboediant. Sed sicut discipulos convenit oboedire magistro, ita et ipsum provide et iuste condecet cuncta disponere.

In omnibus igitur omnes magistram sequentur regulam, neque ab ea temere declinetur a quoquam. Nullus in monasterio proprii sequatur cordis voluntatem. Neque præsumat quisquam cum abbate suo proterve aut foris monasterium contendere. Quod si præsumpserit, regulari disciplinæ subiaceat. Ipse tamen abbas cum timore Dei et observatione regulæ omnia faciat, sciens se procul dubio de omnibus iudiciis suis æquissimo iudici Deo rationem redditurum. Si qua vero minora agenda sunt in monasterii utilitatibus, seniorum tantum utatur consilio, sicut scriptum est: *Omnia fac cum consilio, et post factum non pæniteberis.*

Caput 4: Quæ sunt instrumenta bonorum operum

In primis Dominum Deum diligere ex toto corde, tota anima, tota virtute. Deinde proximum tamquam seipsum. Deinde non occidere. Non adulterare. Non facere futum. Non concupiscere. Non falsum testimonium dicere. Honorare omnes homines. Et quod sibi quis fieri non vult, alio ne faciat. Abnegare semetipsum sibi ut sequatur Christum. Corpus castigare. Delicias non amplecti. Ieiunium amare. Pauperes recreare.Nudum vestire. Infirmum visitare. Mortuum sepelire. In tribulatione subvenire. Dolentem consolari. Sæculi actibus se facere alienum. Nihil amori Christi præponere. Iram non perficere.

Iracundiæ tempus non reservare. Dolum in
corde non tenere. Pacem falsam non dare.
Caritatem non derelinquere. Non iurare ne forte
periuret. Veritatem ex corde et ore proferre.
Malum pro malo non reddere. Iniuriam non
facere, sed et factas patienter sufferre. Inimicos
diligere. Maledicentes se non remaledicere, sed
magis benedicere. Persecutionem pro iustitia
sustinere. Non esse superbum. Non
vinolentum. Non multum edacem. Non
somnulentum. Non pigrum. Non
murmuriosum. Non detractorem. Spem suam
Deo committere. Bonum aliquid in se cum
viderit, Deo adplicet, non sibi. Malum vero
semper a se factum sciat et sibi reputet.

Diem iudicii timere. Gehennam expavescere.
Vitam æternam omni concupiscentia spiritali
desiderare. Mortem cotidie ante oculos
suspectam habere. Actus vitæ suæ omni hora
custodire. In omni loco Deum se respicere pro
certo scire. Cogitationes malas cordi suo
advenientes mox ad Christum adlidere et seniori
spiritali patefacere.Os suum a malo vel pravo
eloquio custodire. Multum loqui non amare.

Verba vana aut risui apta non loqui. Risum multum aut excussum non amare. Lectiones sanctas libenter audire. Orationi frequenter incumbere. Mala sua præterita cum lacrimis vel gemitu cotidie in oratione Deo confiteri. De ipsis malis de cetero emendare. Desideria carnis non efficere. Voluntatem propriam odire. Præceptis abbatis in omnibus oboedire, etiam si ipse aliter - quod absit - agat, memores illud dominicum præceptum: *Quæ dicunt facite, quæ autem faciunt facere nolite.* Non velle dici sanctum antequam sit, sed prius esse quod verius dicatur.

Præcepta Dei factis cotidie adimplere. Castitatem amare. Nullum odire. Zelum non habere. Invidiam non exercere. Contentionem non amare. Elationem fugere. Et seniores venerare. Iuniores diligere. In Christi amore pro inimicis orare. Cum discordante ante solis occasum in pacem redire. Et de Dei misericordia numquam desperare. Ecce hæc sunt instrumenta artis spiritalis. Quæ cum fuerint a nobis die noctuque incessabiliter adimpleta et in die iudicii reconsignata, illa mercis nobis a Domino reconpensabitur quam

ipse promisit: *Quod oculus non vidit nec auris audivit,
quæ præparavit Deus his qui diligunt illum.* Officina
vero ubi hæc omnia diligenter operemur claustra
sunt monasterii et stabilitas in congregatione.

Caput 5: De oboedentia

Primus humilitatis gradus est oboedientia sine
mora. Hæc convenit his qui nihil sibi a Christo
carius aliquid existimant. Propter servitium
sanctum quod professi sunt seu propter metum
gehennæ vel gloriam vitæ æternæ, mox aliquid
imperatum a maiore fuerit, ac si divinitus
imperetur, moram pati nesciant in faciendo. De
quibus Dominus dicit: *Obauditu auris oboedivit
mihi.* Et item dicit doctoribus: *Qui vos audit me
audit.* Ergo hii tales, relinquentes statim quæ sua
sunt et voluntatem propriam deserentes, mox
exoccupatis manibus et quod agebant
imperfectum relinquentes, vicino oboedentiæ
pede iubentis vocem factis sequuntur, et veluti
uno momento prædicta magistri iussio et
perfecta discipuli opera, in velocitate timoris
Dei, ambæ res communiter citius explicantur.
Quibus ad vitam æternam gradiendi amor
incumbit, ideo angustam viam arripiunt, unde

Regula Sanctissimi Patris Benedicti

Dominus dicit: *Angusta via est quæ ducit ad vitam*, ut non suo arbitrio viventes et desideriis suis et voluptatibus oboedientes, sed ambulantes alieno iudicio et imperio, in coenobiis degentes abbatem sibi præesse desiderant. Sine dubio hii tales illam Domini imitantur sententiam qua dicit: *Non veni facere voluntatem meam, sed eius qui misit me.*

Sed hæc ipsa oboedientia tunc acceptabilis erit Deo et dulcis hominibus, si quod iubetur non trepide, non tarde, non tepide, aut cum murmurio vel cum responso nolentis efficiatur, quia oboedientia quæ maioribus præbetur Deo exhibetur; ipse enim dixit: *Qui vos audit me audit.* Et cum bono animo a discipulis præberi oportet, quia *hilarem datorem diligit Deus*. Nam, cum malo animo si oboedit discipulus et non solum ore, sed etiam in corde si murmuraverit, etiam si impleat iussionem, tamen acceptum iam non erit Deo, qui cor eius respicit murmurantem. Et pro tali facto nullam consequitur gratiam, immo poenam murmurantium incurrit, si non cum satisfactione emendaverit.

Caput 6: De taciturnitate

Faciamus quod ait Propheta: *Dixi: custodiam vias meas, ut non delinquam in lingua mea. Posui ori meo custodiam, obmutui et humiliatus sum et silui a bonis.* Hic ostendit Propheta, si a bonis eloquiis interdum propter taciturnitatem debet tacere, quanto magis a malis verbis propter poenam peccati debet cessari. Ergo quamvis de bonis et sanctis et ædificationum eloquiis perfectis discipulis propter taciturnitatis gravitatem rara loquendi concedatur licentia, quia scriptum est:*In multiloquio non effugies peccatum*, et alibi: *Mors et vita in manibus linguæ.* Nam loqui et docere magistrum condecet, tacere et audire discipulum convenit. Et ideo, si qua requirenda sunt a priore, cum omni humilitate et subiectione reverentiæ requirantur. Scurrilitates vero vel verba otiosa et risum moventia æterna clusura in omnibus locis damnamus et ad talia eloquia aperire os non permittimus.

Caput 7: De humilitate

Clamat nobis Scriptura divina, fratres, dicens: *Omnis qui se exaltat humiliabitur et qui se humiliat exaltabitur.* Cum hæc ergo dicit, ostendit nobis omnem exaltationem genus esse superbiæ. Quod se cavere Propheta indicat dicens: *Domine, non est exaltatum cor meum neque elati sunt oculi mei, neque ambulavi in magnis neque in mirabilibus super me.* Sed quid, *si non humiliter sentiebam, si exaltavi animam meam, sicut ablactatum super matrem suam, ita retribues in animam suam.*

Unde fratres, si summæ humilitatis volumus culmen adtingere et ad exaltationem illam cælestem ad quam per præsentis vitæ humilitatem ascenditur, volumus velociter pervenire, actibus nostris ascendentibus scala illa erigenda est quæ in somnio Iacob apparuit, per quam ei descendentes et ascendentes angeli monstrabantur. Non aliud sine dubio descensus ille et ascensus a nobis intelligitur nisi exaltatione descendere et humilitate ascendere. Scala vero ipsa erecta nostra est vita in sæculo, quæ humiliato corde a Domino erigatur ad cælum. Latera enim eius scalæ dicimus nostrum esse corpus et animam, in qua latera diversos gradus humilitatis vel disciplinæ evocatio divina ascendendo inseruit.

Primus itaque humilitatis gradus est, si timorem
Dei sibi ante oculos semper ponens, oblivionem
omnimo fugiat et semper sit memor omnia quæ
præcepit Deus, ut qualiter et contemnentes
Deum gehenna de peccatis incendat et vita
æterna quæ timentibus Deum præparata est,
animo suo semper revolvat. Et custodiens se
omni hora a peccatis et vitiis, id est
cogitationum, linguæ, manuum, pedum vel
voluntatis propriæ sed et desideria , æstimet se
homo de cælis a Deo semper respici omni hora
et facta sua omni loco ab aspectu Divinitatis
videri et ab angelis omni hora renuntiari.
Demonstrans nobis hoc Propheta, cum in
cogitationibus nostris ita Deum semper
præsentem ostendit dicens: *Scrutans corda et renes
Deus*; et item: *Dominus novit cogitationes hominum*; et
item dicit: *Intellexisti cogitationes meas a longe*; et:
Quia cogitatio hominis confitebitur tibi. Nam ut
sollicitus sit circa cogitationes suas perversas,
dicat semper utilis frater in corde suo: *Tunc ero
immaculatus coram eo si observavero me ab iniquitate
mea.*

Voluntatem vero propriam ita facere prohibemur cum dicit Scriptura nobis: *Et a voluntatibus tuis avertere.* Et item rogamus Deum in oratione ut *fiat* illius *voluntas* in nobis. Docemur ergo merito nostram non facere voluntatem cum cavemus illud quod dicit Scriptura: *Sunt viæ quæ putantur ab hominibus rectæ, quarum finis usque ad profundum inferni demergit,* et cum item pavemus illud quod de neglegentibus dictum est: *Corrupti sunt et abominabiles facti sunt in voluntatibus suis.* In desideriis vero carnis ita nobis Deum credamus semper esse præsentem, cum dicit Propheta Domino: *Ante te est omne desiderium meum.*

Cavendum ergo ideo malum desiderium, quia mors secus introitum dilectationis posita est. Unde Scriptura præcepit dicens: *Post concupiscentias tuas non eas.* Ergo si *oculi Domini speculantur bonos et malos* et *Dominus de cælo semper respicit super filios hominum, ut videat si est intellegens aut requirens Deum,* et si ab angelis nobis deputatis cotidie die noctuque Domino factorum nostrorum opera nuntiantur, cavendum est ergo omni hora, fratres, sicut dicit

in psalmo Propheta, ne nos declinantes in malo
et inutiles factos aliqua hora aspiciat Deus et,
parcendo nobis in hoc tempore, quia pius est et
expectat nos converti in melius, ne dicat nobis
in futuro: *Hæc fecisti et tacui.*

Secundus humilitatis gradus est, si propriam
quis non amans voluntatem desideria sua non
delectetur implere, sed vocem illam Domini
factis imitemur dicentis: *Non veni facere voluntatem
meam, sed eius qui me misit.* Item dicit Scriptura:
Voluntas habet poenam et necessitas parit coronam.

Tertius humilitatis gradus est, ut quis pro Dei
amore omni oboedientia se subdat maiori,
imitans Dominum, de quo dicit Apostolus:
Factus oboediens usque ad mortem.

Quartus humulitatis gradus est, si in ipsa
oboedientia duris et contrariis rebus vel etiam
quibuslibet inrogatis iniuriis, tacite conscientia
patientiam amplectatur et sustinens non
lassescat vel discedat, dicente Scriptura: *Qui
perseveraverit usque in finem, hic salvus erit.* Item:
Confortetur cor tuum et sustine Dominum. Et
ostendens fidelem pro Domino universa etiam

contraria sustinere debere, dicit ex persona
sufferentium: *Propter te morte adficimur tota die,
æstimati sumus ut oves occisionis.* Et securi de spe
retributionis divinæ subsecuntur gaudentes et
dicentes: *Sed in his omnibus superamus propter eum
qui dilexit nos.* Et item alio loco Scriptura: *Probasti
nos, Deus, igne nos examinasti sicut igne examinatur
argentum; induxisti nos in laqueum; posuisti
tribulationes in dorso nostro.* Et ut ostendat sub
priore debere nos esse, subsequitur dicens:
Inposuisti homines super capita nostra. Sed et
præceptum Domini in adversis et iniuriis per
patientiam adimplentes, qui *percussi in maxillam
præbent et aliam, auferenti* tunicam *dimittunt et
pallium, angarizati militario vadunt duo,* cum Paulo
apostolo *falsos fratres* sustinent et *persecutionem
sustinent,* et *maledicentes* se *benedicent.*

Quintus humilitatis gradus est, si omnes
cogitationes malas cordi suo advenientes vel
mala a se absconse commissa per humilem
confessionem abbatem non celaverit suum.
Hortans nos de hac re Scriptura dicens: *Revela ad
Dominum viam tuam et spera in eum.* Et item dicit:
Confitemini Domino quoniam bonus, quoniam in

æternum misericordia eius. Et item Propheta:
Delictum meum cognitum tibi feci et iniustitias meas non operui. Dixi: pronuntiabo adversum me iniustitias meas Domino, et tu remisisti impietatem cordis mei.

Sextus humilitatis gradus est, si omni vilitate vel extremitate contentus sit monachus, et ad omnia quæ sibi iniunguntur velut operarium malum se iudicet et indignum, dicens sibi cum Propheta:
Ad nihilum redactus sum et nescivi; ut iumentum factus sum apud te et ego semper tecum.

Septimus humilitatis gradus est: si omnibus se inferiorem et viliorem non solum sua lingua pronuntiet, sed etiam intimo cordis credat affectu, humilians se et dicens cum Propheta:
Ego autem sum vermis et non homo, obprobrium hominum et abiectio plebis. Exaltatus sum et humiliatus et confusus. Et item: *Bonum mihi quod humiliasti me, et discam mandata tua.*

Octavus humilitatis gradus est, si nihil agat monachus, nisi quod communis monasterii regula vel maiorum cohortatur exempla.

Nonus humilitatis gradus est, si linguam ad loquendum prohibeat monachus et taciturnitatem habens, usque ad interrogationem non loquatur, monstrante Scriptura quia *in multoloquio non effugitur peccatum*, et quia *vir linguosus non dirigitur super terram.*

Decimus humilitatis gradus est, si non sit facilis ac promptus in risu, qui scriptum est: *Stultus in risu exaltat vocem suam.*

Undecimus humilitatis gradus est, si cum loquitur monachus, leniter et sine risu, humiliter cum gravitate vel pauca verba et rationabilia loquatur, et non sit clamosus in voce, sicut scriptum est: *Sapiens verbis innotescit paucis.*

Duodecimus humilitatis gradus est, si non solum corde monachus, sed etiam ipso corpore humilitatem videntibus se semper indicet, id est Opere Dei, in oratorio, in monasterio, in horto, in via, in agro vel ubicumque sedens, ambulans vel stans, inclinato sit semper capite, defixis in terram aspectibus, reum se omni hora de peccatis suis æstimans iam se tremendo iudicio repræsentari æstimet, dicens sibi in corde

semper illud, quod publicanus ille evangelicus
fixis in terram oculis dixit: *Domine, non sum
dignus, ego peccator, levare oculos meos ad cælos.* Et
item cum Propheta: *Incurvatus sum et humiliatus
sum usquequaque.* Ergo, his omnibus humilitatis
gradibus ascensis, monachus mox ad caritatem
Dei perveniet illam quæ perfecta foris mittit
timorem, per quam universa quæ prius non sine
formidine observabat absque ullo labore velut
naturaliter ex consuetudine incipiet custodire,
non iam timore gehennæ, sed amore Christi et
consuetudine ipsa bona et dilectatione virtutum.
Quæ Dominus iam in operarium suum
mundum a vitiis et peccatis Spiritu Sancto
dignabitur demonstrare.

Caput 8: De officiis divinis in noctibus

Hiemis tempore, id est a kalendas novembres
usque in Pascha, iuxta considerationem rationis,
octava hora noctis surgendum est, ut modice
amplius de media nocte pausetur et iam digesti
surgant. Quod vero restat post Vigilias a
fratribus qui psalterii vel lectionum aliquid
indigent, meditationi inserviatur. A Pascha
autem usque ad supradictas novembres sic

temperetur hora, ut Vigiliarum agenda
parvissimo intervallo, quo fratres ad necessaria
naturæ exeant, mox Matutini qui incipiente luce
agendi sunt, subsequantur.

Caput 9: Quanti psalmi dicendi sunt nocturni

Hiemis tempore suprascripto, in primis versu
tertio dicendum: *Domine, labia mea aperies, et os
meum adnuntiabit laudem tuam.* Cum subiungendus
est tertius psalmus et Gloria. Post hunc,
psalmum nonagesimum quartum cum antefana,
aut certe decantandum. Inde sequatur
ambrosianum, deinde sex psalmi cum antefanas.
Quibus dictis, dicto versu, benedicat abbas et,
sedentibus omnibus in scamnis, legantur
vicissim a fratribus in codice super analogium
tres lectiones, inter quas et tria responsoria
cantentur. Duo responsoria sine Gloria
dicantur; post tertiam vero lectionem, qui cantat
dicat Gloriam. Quam dum incipit cantor dicere,
mox omnes de sedilia sua surgant ob honorem
et reverentiam sanctæ Trinitatis. Codices autem
legantur in Vigiliis divinæ auctoritatis tam
Veteris Testamenti quam Novi, sed et

expositiones earum, quæ a nominatis et
orthodoxis catholicis Patribus factæ sunt. Post
has vero tres lectiones cum responsoria sua,
sequantur reliqui sex psalmi cum Alleluia
canendi. Post hos, lectio Apostoli sequatur ex
corde recitanda, et versus, et supplicatio litaniæ,
id est Quirie eleison. Et sic finiantur Vigiliæ
nocturnæ.

Caput 10: Qualiter æstatis tempore agatur nocturna laus

A Pascha autem usque ad kalendas novembres,
omnis ut supra dictum est psalmodiæ quantitas
teneatur excepto quod lectiones in codice
propter brevitatem noctium legantur, sed pro
ipsis tribus lectionibus una de Veteri
Testamento memoriter dicatur, quam brevis
responsorius subsequatur. Et reliqua omnia, ut
dictum est, impleantur, id est ut numquam
minus a duodecim psalmorum quantitate ad
Vigilias nocturnas dicantur, exceptis tertio et
nonagesimo quarto psalmo.

Caput 11: Qualiter diebus dominicis vigiliæ agantur

Dominico die temperius surgatur ad Vigilias. In quibus Vigiliis teneatur mensura, id est, modulatis ut supra disposuimus sex psalmis et versu, residentibus cunctis disposite et per ordinem in subselliis, legantur in codice, ut supra diximus, quattuor lectiones cum responsoriis suis. Ubi tantum in quarto responsorio dicatur a cantante Gloria; quam dum incipit, mox omnes cum reverentia surgant. Post quibus lectionibus sequantur ex ordine alii sex psalmi cum antefanas sicut anteriores, et versu. Post quibus iterum legantur aliæ quattuor lectiones cum responsoriis suis, ordine quo supra. Post quibus dicantur tria cantica Prophetarum, quas instituerit abbas; quæ cantica cum Alleluia psallantur. Dicto etiam versu et benedicente abbate, legantur aliæ quattuor lectiones de Novo Testamento, ordine quo supra. Post quartum autem responsorium incipiat abbas hymnum Te Deum laudamus. Quo perdicto, legat abbas lectionem de Evangelia, cum honore et timore stantibus omnibus. Qua perlecta, respondeant omnes

Amen, et subsequatur mox abbas hymnum Te
decet laus, et data benedictione incipiant
Matutinos. Qui ordo Vigiliarum omni tempore
tam æstatis quam hiemis æqualiter in die
dominico teneatur, nisi forte - quod absit -
tardius surgant, aliquid de lectionibus
breviandum est aut responsoriis. Quod tamen
omnino caveatur ne proveniat; quod si
contigerit, digne inde satisfaciat Deo in oratorio
per cuius evenerit neglectum.

Caput 12: Quomodo matutinorum sollemnitas agatur

In Matutinis dominico die, in primis dicatur
sexagesimus sextus psalmus, sine antefana, in
directum. Post quem dicatur quinquagesimus
cum Alleluia. Post quem dicatur centisemus
septimus decimus et sexagesimus secundus.
Inde Benectiones et Laudes, lectionem de
Apocalipsis una ex corde et responsorium,
ambrosianum, versu, canticum de Evangelia,
litania, et conpletum est.

Caput 13: Privatis diebus qualiter agantur matutini

Diebus autem privatis Matutinorum sollemnitas ita agatur, id est, ut sexagesimus sextus psalmus sine antefana, subtrahendo modice, sicut Dominica, ut omnes occurant ad quinquagesimum, qui cum antefana dicatur. Post quem alii duo psalmi dicantur secundum consuetudinem, id est: secunda feria quintus et tricesimus quintus; tertia feria quadragesimus secundus et quinquagesimus sextus; quarta feria sexagesimum tertium et sexagesimum quartum; quinta feria octogesimum septimum et octogesimum nonum; sexta feria septuagesimum quintum et nonagesimum primum; sabbatorum autem centesimum quadragesimum secundum et canticum Deuteronomium, qui dividatur in duas Glorias. Nam ceteris diebus canticum unumquemque die suo ex Prophetis, sicut psallit Ecclesia romana, dicantur. Post hæc sequantur Laudes; deinde lectio una Apostoli memoriter recitanda, responsorium, ambrosianum, versu, canticum de Evangelia, litania et conpletum est. Plane agenda matutina vel vespertina non transeat

aliquando, nisi in ultimo per ordinem oratio
dominica, omnibus audientibus, dicatur a priore
propter scandalorum spinas quæ oriri solent, ut
conventi per ipsius orationis sponsionem qua
dicunt: *Dimitte nobis sicut et nos dimittimus*, purgent
se ab huiusmodi vitio. Ceteris vero agendis
ultima pars eius orationis dicatur, ut ab omnibus
respondeatur: *Sed libera nos a malo.*

Caput 14: In nataliciis sanctorum qualiter agantur vigiliæ

In sanctorum vero festivitatibus vel omnibus
sollemnitatibus sicut diximus dominico die
agendum, ita agatur, excepto quod psalmi aut
antefanæ vel lectiones ad ipsum diem
pertinentes dicantur; modus autem
suprascriptus teneatur.

Caput 15: Alleluia quibus temporibus dicatur

A sanctum Pascha usque Pentecosten sine
intermissione dicatur Alleluia, tam in psalmis
quam in responsoriis. A Pentecosten autem
usque caput quadragesimæ, omnibus noctis,
cum sex posterioribus psalmis tantum ad

Nocturnos dicatur. Omni vero Dominica extra quadragesima cantica, Matutinos, Prima, Tertia, Sexta Nonaque cum Alleluia dicatur, Vespera vero iam antefana. Responsoria vero numquam dicantur cum Alleluia, nisi a Pascha usque Pentecosten.

Caput 16: Qualiter divina opera per diem agantur

Ut ait Propheta: *Septies in die laudem dixi tibi.* Qui septenarius sacratus numerus a nobis sic implebitur, si Matutino, Primæ, Tertiæ, Sextæ, Nonæ, Vesperæ Conpletoriique tempore nostræ servitutis officia persolvamus, quia de his diurnis Horis dixit: *Septies in die laudem dixi tibi.* Nam de nocturnis Vigiliis idem ipse Propheta ait: *Media nocte surgebam ad confitendum tibi.* Ergo his temporibus referamus laudes Creatori nostro super iudicia iustitiæ suæ, id est Matutinis, Prima, Tertia, Sexta, Nona, Vespera, Conpletorios, et nocte surgamus ad confitendum ei.

Caput 17: Quot psalmi per easdem horas dicendi sunt

Iam de Nocturnis vel Matutinis digessimus ordinem psalmodiæ; nunc de sequentibus Horis videamus. Prima hora dicantur psalmi tres singillatim et non sub una Gloria, hymnum eiusdem Horæ post versum Deus, in adiutorium, antequam psalmi incipiantur. Post expletionem vero trium psalmorum recitetur lectio una, versu et Quirie eleison et missas. Tertia vero, Sexta et Nona item eo ordine celebretur oratio, id est versu, hymnos earundem Horarum, ternos psalmos, lectionem et versu, Quirie eleison et missas. Si maior congregatio fuerit, cum antefanas, si vero minor, in directum psallantur. Vespertina autem sinaxis quattuor psalmis cum antefanas terminetur. Post quibus psalmis lectio recitanda est: inde responsorium, ambrosianum, versu, canticum de Evangelia, litania, et oratione dominica fiant missæ. Conpletorios autem trium psalmorum dictione terminentur; qui psalmi directanei sine antefana dicendi sunt. Post quos hymnum eiusdem Horæ, lectionem unam, versu, Quirie eleison, et benedictione missæ fiant.

Caput 18: Quo ordine ipsi psalmi dicendi sunt

In primis dicatur versu: *Deus, in adiutorium meum intende; Domine, ad adiuvandum me festina*, Gloria, inde hymnum unuscuiusque Horæ. deinde Prima Hora, Dominica, dicenda quattuor capitula psalmi centesimi octavi decimi. Reliquis vero Horis, id est Tertia, Sexta vel Nona, terna capitula suprascripti psalmi centesimi octavi decimi dicantur. Ad Primam autem secundæ feriæ dicantur tres psalmi, id est primus, secundus et sextus. Et ita per singulos dies ad Primam, usque Dominica, dicantur per ordinem terni psalmi usque nonum decimum psalmum, ita sane, ut nonus psalmus et septimus decimus partiantur in binos. Et sic fit, ut ad Vigilias Dominica semper a vicesimo incipiatur.

Ad Tertiam vero, Sextam Nonamque secundæ feriæ novem capitula quæ residua sunt de centesimo octavo decimo, ipsa terna per easdem Horas dicantur. Expenso ergo psalmo centesimo ocatvo decimo duobus diebus, id est Dominico et secunda feria, tertia feria iam ad Tertiam, Sextam vel Nonam psallantur terni

psalmi a centesimo nono decimo usque
centesimo vicesimo septimo, id est psalmi
novem. Quique psalmi semper usque Dominica
per easdem Horas itidem repetantur, hymnorum
nihilominus, lectionum vel versuum
dispositionem uniformem cunctis diebus
servatam. Et ita scilicet semper Dominica a
centesimo octavo decimo incipietur.

Vespera autem cotidie quattuor psalmorum
modulatione canatur. Qui psalmi incipiantur a
centesimo nono usque centesimo quadragesimo
septimo, exceptis his qui in diversis Horis ex eis
sequestrantur, id est a centesimo septimo
decimo usque centesimo vicesimo septimo et
centesimo tricesimo tertio et centesimo
quadragesimo secundo; reliqui omnes in
Vespera dicendi sunt. Et quia minus veniunt
tres psalmi, ideo dividendi sunt qui ex numero
suprascripto fortiores inveniuntur, id est
centesimum tricesimum octavum et centesimum
quadragesimum tertium et centesimum
quadragesimum quartum; centesimus vero
sextus decimus, quia parvus est, cum centesimo
quinto decimo coniungatur. Digesto ergo ordine

psalmorum vespertinorum, reliquia, id est lectionem, responsum, hymnum, versum vel canticum, sicut supra taxavimus impleatur. Ad Conpletorios vero cotidie idem psalmi repetantur, id est quartum, nonagesimum et centesimum tricesimum tertium.

Disposito ordine psalmodiæ diurnæ, reliqui omnes psalmi qui supersunt æqualiter dividantur in septem noctium Vigilias, partiendoscilicet qui inter eos prolixiores sunt psalmi et duodecim per unamquamque constituens noctem. Hoc præcipue commonentes ut, si sui forte hæc distributio psalmorum displicuerit, ordinet si melius aliter iudicaverit, dum omnimodis id adtendat, ut omni ebdomada psalterium ex integro numero centum quinquaginta psalmorum psallantur, et dominico die semper a caput reprendatur ad Vigilias. Quia nimis inertem devotionis suæ servitium ostendunt monachi qui minus a psalterio cum canticis consuetudinariis per septimanæ circulum psallunt, dum quando legamus sanctos Patres nostros uno die hoc strenue implesse, quod nos tepidi utinam septimana integra persolvamus.

Caput 19: De disciplina psallendi

Ubique credimus divinam esse præsentiam et
oculos Domini in omni loco speculari bonos et malos,
maxime tamen hoc sine aliqua dubitatione
credamus, cum ad opus divinum adsistimus.
Ideo semper memores simus quod ait Propheta:
Servite Domino in timore, et iterum: *Psallite sapienter,*
et: *In conspectu angelorum psallam tibi.* Ergo
consideremus qualiter oporteat in conspectu
Divinitatis et angelorum eius esse, et sic stemus
ad psallendum, ut mens nostra concordet voci
nostræ.

Caput 20: De reverentia orationis

Si, cum hominibus potentibus volumus aliqua
suggerere, non præsumimus nisi cum humilitate
et reverentia, quanto magis Domino Deo
universorum cum omni humilitate et puritatis
devotione supplicandum est. Et non in
multiloquio, sed in puritate cordis et
conpunctione lacrimarum nos exaudiri sciamus.
Et ideo brevis debet esse et pura oratio, nisi
forte ex affectu inspirationis divinæ gratiæ
protendatur. In conventu tamen omnino

brevietur oratio, et facto signo a priore pariter surgant.

Caput 21: De decanis monasterii

Si maior fuerit congregatio, elegantur de ipsis fratres boni testimonii et sanctæ conversationis, et constituantur decani, qui sollicitudinem gerant super decanias suas in omnibus secundum mandata Dei et præcepta abbatis sui. Qui decani tales elegantur in quibus securus abbas partiat onera sua. Et non elegantur per ordinem, sed secundum vitæ meritum et sapientiæ doctrinam. Quique decani, si ex eis aliqua forte qui inflatus superbia repertus fuerit reprehensibilis, correptus semel et iterum atque tertio si emendare noluerit, deiciatur, et alter in loco eius qui dignus est subrogetur. Et de præposito eadem constituimus.

Caput 22: Quomodo dormiant monachi

Singuli per singula lecta dormiant. Lectisternia pro modo conversationis secundum dispensationem abbatis sui accipiant. Si potest fieri omnes in uno loco dormiant; sin autem multitudo non sinit, deni aut viceni cum

senioribus qui super eos solliciti sint, pausent.
Candela iugiter in eadem cella ardeat usque
mane. Vestiti dormiant et cincti cingulis aut
funibus, ut cultellos suos ad latus suum non
habeant dum dormiunt, ne forte per somnium
vulnerent dormientem; et ut parati sint monachi
semper et, facto signo absque mora surgentes,
festinent invicem se prævenire ad opus Dei,
cum omni tamen gravitate et modestia.
Adulescentiores fratres iuxta se non habeant
lectos, sed permixti cum senioribus. Surgentes
vero ad opus Dei invicem se moderate
cohortentur propter somnulentorum
excusationes.

Caput 23: De excommunicatione culparum

Si quis frater contumax aut inoboediens aut
superbus aut murmurans vel in aliquo contrarius
sanctæ regulæ et præceptis seniorum suorum
contemptor repertus fuerit, hic secundum
Domini nostri præceptum admoneatur semel et
secundo secrete a senioribus suis. Si non
emendaverit, obiurgetur publice coram
omnibus. Si vero neque sic correxerit, si
intelligit qualis poena sit, excommunicationi

subiaceat; sin autem inprobus est, vindictæ corporali subdatur.

Caput 24: Qualis debet esse modus excommunicationis

Secundum modum culpæ, et excommunicationis vel disciplinæ mensura debet extendi. Qui culparum modus in abbatis pendat iudicio. Si quis tamen frater in levioribus culpis invenitur, a mensæ participatione privetur. Privati autem a mensæ consortio ista erit ratio, ut in oratorio psalmum aut antefanam non imponat, neque lectionem recitet, usque ad satisfactionem. Refectionem autem cibi post fratrum refectionem solus accipiat, ut, si verbi gratia fratres reficiunt sexta hora, ille frater nona, si fratres nona, ille vespera, usque dum satisfactione congrua veniam consequatur.

Caput 25: De gravioribus culpis

Is autem frater qui gravioribus culpæ noxa tenetur, suspendatur a mensa, simul ab oratorio. Nullus ei fratrum in nullo iungatur consortio nec in conloquio. Solus sit ad opus sibi iniunctum, persistens in pænitentiæ luctu, sciens

illam terribilem Apostoli sententiam dicentis:
*Traditum eiusmodi hominem in interitum carnis, ut
spiritus salvus sit in diem Domini.* Cibi autem
refectionem solus percipiat, mensura vel hora
qua præviderit abbas ei conpetere; nec a
quoquam benedicatur transeunte nec cibum
quod ei datur.

Caput 26: De his qui sine iussione iungunt se excommunicatis

Si quis frater præsumpserit sine iussione abbatis
fratri excommunicato quolibet modo se iungere
aut loqui cum eo vel mandatum ei dirigere,
similem sortiatur excommunicationis vindictam.

Caput 27: Qualiter debeat abbas sollicitus esse circa excommunicatos

Omni sollicitudine curam gerat abbas circa
delinquentes fratres, quia: *Non est opus sanis
medicus, sed male habentibus.* Et ideo uti debet
omni modo ut sapiens medicus: inmittere
senpectas, id est seniores sapientes fratres, qui
quasi secrete consolentur fratrem fluctuantem et
provocent ad humilitatis satisfactionem et
consolentur eum ne abundantiori tristitia

absorbeatur, sed, sicut ait item Apostolus: *Confirmetur in eo caritas*, et oretur pro eo ab omnibus. Magnopere enim debet sollicitudinem gerere abbas et omni sagacitate et industria currere, ne aliquam de ovibus sibi creditis perdat. Noverit enim se infirmarum curam suscepisse animarum, non super sanas tyrannidem. Et metuat Prophetæ comminationem per quam dicit Deus: *Quod crassum videbatis, et quod debile erat proiciebatis.* Et Pastoris boni pium imitetur exemplum, qui, relictis nonaginta novem ovibus in montibus, abiit unam ovem quæ erraverat quærere. Cuius infirmati in tantum conpassus est, ut eam in sacris humeris suis dignaretur inponere et sic reportare ad gregem.

Caput 28: De his qui sæpius correpti emendare noluerint

Si quis frater frequenter correptus pro qualibet culpa, si etiam excommunicatus non emendaverit, acrior ei accedat correptio, id est ut verberum vindicta in eum procedant. Quod si nec ita correxerit, aut forte - quod absit - in superbia elatus etiam defendere voluerit opera

sua, tunc abbas faciat quod sapiens medicus: si
exhibuit fomenta, si unguenta adhortationum, si
medicamina Scripturarum divinarum, si ad
ultimum ustionem excommunicationis vel
plagarum virgæ, et iam si viderit nihil suam
prævalere industriam, adhibeat etiam, quod
maius est, suam et omnium fratrum pro eo
orationem, ut Dominus qui omnia potest
operetur salutem circa infirmum fratrem. Quod
si nec isto modo sanatus fuerit, tunc iam utatur
abbas ferro abscisionis, ut ait Apostolus: *Auferte
malum ex vobis*; et iterum: *Infidelis si discedit,
discedat*, ne una ovis morbida omnem gregem
contagiet.

Caput 29: Si debeant fratres exeuntes de monasterio item recipi

Frater qui proprio vitio egreditur de monasterio,
si reverti voluerit, spondeat prius omnem
emendationem pro quo egressus est, et sic in
ultimo gradu recipiatur, ut ex hoc eius humilitas
conprobetur. Quod si denuo exierit, usque
tertio ita recipiatur, iam postea sciens omnem
sibi reversionis aditum denegari.

Caput 30: De pueris minori ætate qualiter corripiantur

Omnis ætas vel intellectus proprias debet habere mensuras. Ideoque quotiens pueri vel adulescentiores ætate, aut qui minus intellegere possunt, quanta poena sit excommunicationis, hii tales dum delinquunt, aut ieiuniis nimiis affligantur aut acris verberibus coerceantur, ut sanentur.

Caput 31: De cellarario monasterii qualis sit

Cellararius monasterii elegatur de congregatione sapiens, maturis moribus, sobrius, non multum edax, non elatus, non turbulentus, non iniuriosus, non tardus, non prodigus, sed timens Deum; qui omni congregationi sit sicut pater. Curam gerat de omnibus. Sine iussione abbatis nihil faciat. Quæ iubentur custodiat. Fratres non contristet. Si quis frater ab eo foret aliqua inrationabiliter postulat, non spernendo eum contristet, sed rationabiliter cum humilitate male petenti deneget. Animam suam custodiat, memor semper illud apostolicum, quia: *Qui bene ministraverit, gradum bonum sibi adquirit.*

Regula Sanctissimi Patris Benedicti

Infirmorum, infantum, hospitum pauperumque cum omni sollicitudine curam gerat, sciens sine dubio, quia pro his omnibus in die iudicii rationem redditurus est. Omnia vasa monasterii cunctamque substantiam ac si altaris vasa sacrata conspiciat. Nihil ducat neglegendum. Neque avaritiæ studeat neque prodigus sit et stirpator substantiæ monasterii, sed omnia mensurate faciat et secundum iussionem abbatis.

Humilitatem ante omnia habeat, et cui substantia non est quod tribuatur, sermo responsionis porrigatur bonus, ut scriptum est: *Sermo bonus super datum optimum.* Omnia quæ ei iniunxerit abbas, ipsa habeat sub cura sua; a quibus eum prohibuerit, non præsumat. Fratribus constitutam annonam sine aliquo tyfo vel mora offerat, ut non scandalizentur, memor divini eloquii, quid mereatur *qui scandalizaverit unum de pusillis.* Si congregatio maior fuerit, solacia ei dentur, a quibus adiutus et ipse æquo animo impleat officium sibi commissum. Horis conpetentibus et dentur quæ danda sunt et

petantur quæ petanda sunt, nemo perturbetur
neque contristetur in domo Dei.

Caput 32: De ferramentis vel rebus monasterii

Substantia monasterii in ferramentis vel vestibus
seu quibuslibet rebus prævideat abbas fratres de
quorum vita et moribus securus sit; et eis
singula, ut utile iudicaverit, consignet
custodienda atque recolligenda. Ex quibus abbas
brevem teneat, ut dum sibi in ipsa adsignata
fratres vicissim succedunt, sciat quid dat aut
quid recipit. Si quis autem sordide aut
neglegenter res monasterii tractaverit,
corripiatur; si non emendaverit, disciplinæ
regulari subiaceat.

Caput 33: Si quid debeant monachi proprium habere

Præcipue hoc vitium radicitus amputandum est
de monasterio ne quis præsumat aliquid dare aut
accipere sine iussione abbatis, neque aliquid
habere proprium, nullam omnimo rem, neque
codicem, neque tabulas, neque grafium, sed nihil
omnimo, quippe quibus nec corpora sua nec

voluntates licet habere in propria voluntate;
omnia vero necessaria a patre sperare
monasterii, nec quicquam liceat habere quod
abbas non dederit aut permiserit. *Omniaque
omnibus sint communia*, ut scriptum est, *ne quisquam
suum aliquid dicat* vel præsumat. Quod si
quisquam huic nequissimo vitio deprehensus
fuerit delectari, admoneatur semel et iterum; si
non emendaverit, correptioni subiaceat.

Caput 34: Si omnes æqualiter debeant necessaria accipere

Sicut scriptum est: *Dividebatur singulis prout cuique
opus erat.* Ubi non dicimus ut personarum - quod
absit - acceptio sit, sed infirmitatum
consideratio; ubi qui minus indiget, agat Deo
gratias et non contristetur, qui vero plus indiget,
humilietur pro infirmitate, non extollatur pro
misericordia; et ita omnia membra erunt in pace.
Ante omnia, ne murmurationis malum pro
qualicumque causa in aliquo qualicumque verbo
vel significatione appareat. Quod si deprehensus
fuerit, districtiori disciplinæ subdatur.

Caput 35: De septimanariis coquinæ

Fratres sibi invicem serviant, ut nullus excusetur a coquinæ officio, nisi aut ægritudo aut in causa gravis utilitatis quis occupatus fuerit, quia exinde maior mercis et caritas adquiritur. Inbecillibus autem procurentur solacia, ut non cum tristitia hoc faciant; sed habeant omnes solacia, secundum modum congregationis aut positionem loci. Si maior congregatio fuerit, cellararius excusetur a coquina, vel si qui, ut diximus, maioribus utilitatibus occupantur. Ceteri sibi sub caritate invicem serviant. Egressurus de septimana, sabbato munditias faciat. Lintea cum quibus sibi fratres manus aut pedes tergunt, lavent. Pedes vero tam ipse qui egreditur quam ille qui intraturus est omnibus lavent. Vasa ministerii sui munda et sana cellarario reconsignet; qui cellararius item intranti consignet, ut sciat quod dat aut quod recipit.

Septimanarii autem ante unam horam refectionis accipiant super statutam annonam singulas biberes et panem, ut hora refectionis sine murmuratione et gravi labore serviant

fratribus suis. In diebus tamen sollemnibus
usque ad missas sustineant. Intrantes et
exeuntes ebdomadarii in oratorio mox Matutinis
finitis Dominica omnium genibus provolvantur
postulantes pro se orari. Egrediens autem de
septimana dicat hunc versum: *Benedictus es,
Domine Deus, qui adiuvisti me et consolatus es me.*
Quo dicto tertio accepta benedictione egrediens,
subsequatur ingrediens et dicat: *Deus, in
adiutorium meum intende, Domine, ad adiuvandum me
festina,* et hoc idem tertio repetatur ab omnibus
et accepta benedictione ingrediatur.

Caput 36: De infirmis fratribus

Infirmorum cura ante omnia et super omnia
adhibenda est, ut sicut revera Christo ita eis
serviatur, quia ipse dixit: *Infirmus fui, et visitastis
me,* et: *Quod fecistis uni de his minimis, mihi fecistis.*
Sed et ipsi infirmi considerent in honorem Dei
sibi serviri, et non superfluitate sua contristent
fratres suos servientes sibi; qui tamen patienter
portandi sunt, quia de talibus copiosior mercis
adquiritur. Ergo cura maxima sit abbati, ne
aliquam neglegentiam patiantur. Quibus
fratribus infirmis sit cella super se deputata et

servitor timens Deum et diligens ac sollicitus.
Balnearum usus infirmis quotiens expedit
offeratur, sanis autem et maxime iuvenibus
tardius concedatur. Sed et carnium esus infirmis
omnimo debilibus pro reparatione concedatur;
at ubi meliorati fuerint, a carnibus more solito
omnes abstineant. Curam autem maximam
habeat abbas ne a cellarariis aut a servitoribus
neglegantur infirmi; et ipsum respicit quidquid a
discipulis delinquitur.

Caput 37: De senibus vel infantibus

Licet ipsa natura humana trahatur ad
misericordiam in his ætatibus, senum videlicet et
infantum, tamen et regulæ auctoritas eis
prospiciat. Consideretur semper in eis
inbecillitas et ullatenus eis districtio regulæ
teneatur in alimentis; sed sit in eis pia
consideratio et præveniant horas canonicas.

Caput 38: De ebdomadario lectore

Mensis fratrum lectio deesse non debet, nec
fortuito casu qui arripuerit codicem legere ibi,
sed lecturus tota ebdomada dominica
ingrediatur. Qui ingrediens post missas et

communionem petat ab omnibus pro se orari,
ut avertat ab ipso Deus spiritum elationis. Et
dicatur hic versus in oratorio tertio ab omnibus,
ipso tamen incipiente: *Domine, labia mea aperies, et
os meum adnuntiabit laudem tuam.* Et sic accepta
benedictione ingrediatur ad legendum. Et
summum fiat silentium, ut nullus musitatio vel
vox nisi solius legentis ibi audiatur. Quæ vero
necessaria sunt comedentibus et bibentibus sic
sibi vicissim ministrent fratres, ut nullus indigeat
petere aliquid. Si quid tamen opus fuerit, sonitu
cuiuscumque signi potius petatur quam voce.
Nec præsumat ibi aliquis de ipsa lectione aut
aliunde quicquam requirere, ne detur occasio;
nisi forte prior pro ædificatione voluerit aliquid
breviter dicere. Frater autem lector
ebdomadarius accipiat mixtum, priusquam
incipiat legere, propter communionem sanctam,
et ne forte grave si ei ieiunium sustinere. Postea
autem cum coquinæ ebdomadariis et
servitoribus reficiat. Fratres autem non per
ordinem legant aut cantent, sed qui ædificant
audientes.

Caput 39: De mensura cibus

Sufficere credimus ad refectionem cotidianam tam sextæ quam nonæ, omnibus mensis, cocta duo pulmentaria propter diversorum infirmitatibus, ut forte qui ex illo non potuerit edere, ex alio reficiatur. Ergo duo pulmentaria cocta fratribus omnibus sufficiant et, si fuerit unde poma aut nascentia leguminum, addatur et tertium. Panis libra una propensa sufficiat in die, sive una sit refectio sivi prandii et cenæ. Quod si cenaturi sunt, de eadem libra tertia pars a cellarario servetur reddenda cenandis. Quod si labor forte factus fuerit maior, in arbitrio et potestate abbatis erit, si expediat, aliquid augere, remota præ omnibus crapula, et ut numquam subripiat monacho indigeries; quia nihil sic contrarium est omni christiano quomodo crapula, sicut ait Dominus noster: *Videte ne graventur corda vestra crapula*. Pueris vero minori ætate non eadem servetur quantitas, sed minor quam maioribus, servata in omnibus parcitate. Carnium vero quadrupedum omnimodo ab omnibus abstineatur comestio, præter omnimo debiles ægrotos.

Caput 40: De mensura potus

Unusquisque proprium habet donum ex Deo, alius sic, alius vero sic; et ideo cum aliqua scrupulositate a nobis mensura victus aliorum constituitur. Tamen infirmorum contuentes inbecillitatem, credimus eminam vini per singulos sufficere per diem. Quibus autem donat Deus tolerantiam abstinentiæ, propriam se habituros mercedem sciant. Quod si aut loci necessitas vel labor aut ardor æstatis amplius poposcerit, in arbitrio prioris consistat, considerans in omnibus ne subrepat satietas aut ebrietas. Licet legamus: *Vinum omnimo monachorum non esse*, sed quia nostris temporibus id monachis persuaderi non potest, saltim vel hoc consentiamus ut non usque ad satietatem bibamus, sed parcius, quia: *Vinum apostatare facit etiam sapientes*. Ubi autem necessitas loci exposcit, ut nec suprascripta mensura inveniri possit, sed multo minus aut ex toto nihil, benedicant Deum qui ibi habitant et non murmurent, hoc ante omnia admonentes, ut absque murmurationibus sint.

Caput 41: Quibus horis oportet reficere fratres

A sancto Pascha usque Pentecosten ad sextam reficiant fratres et sera cenent. A Pentecosten autem tota æstate, si labores agrorum non habent monachi aut nimietas æstatis non perturbat, quarta et sexta feria ieiunent usque ad nonam; reliquis diebus ad sextam prandeant. Quam prandii sextam, si operis in agris habuerint aut æstatis fervor nimius fuerit, continuanda erit et in abbatis sit providentia. Et sic omnia temperet atque disponat, qualiter et animæ salventur et quod faciunt fratres absque iusta murmuratione faciant. Ab idus autem septembres usque caput quadragesimæ ad nonam semper reficiant. In quadragesima vero usque in Pascha ad vesperam reficiant. Ipsa tamen Vespera sic agatur, ut lucernæ lumen non indigeant reficientes, sed luce adhuc diei omnia consummentur. Sed et omni tempore, sive cena sive refectionis hora sic temperetur, ut luce fiant omnia.

Caput 42: Ut post conpletorium nemo loquatur

Omni tempore silentium debent studere monachi, maxime tamen nocturnis horis. Et ideo omni tempore, sive ieiunii sive prandii: si tempus fuerit prandii, mox surrexerint a cena, sedeant omnes in unum, et legat unus Collationes vel Vitas Patrum aut certe aliud quod ædificet audientes, non autem Eptaticum aut Regum, quia infirmis intellectibus non erit utile illa hora hanc Scripturam audire, aliis vero horis legantur. Si autem ieiunii dies fuerit, dicta Vespera, parvo intervallo mox accedant ad lectionem Collationum, ut diximus. Et lectis quattuor aut quinque foliis vel quantum hora permittit, omnibus in unum occurentibus per hanc moram lectionis, si qui forte in adsignato sibi commisso fuit occupatus, omnes ergo in unum positi conpleant, et exeuntes a Conpletoriis nulla sit licentia denuo cuiquam loqui aliquid. Quod si inventus fuerit quisquam prævaricare hanc taciturnitatis regulam, gravi vindictæ subiaceat, excepto si necessitas hospitum supervenerit aut forte abbas alicui aliquid iusserit. Quod tamen et ipsud cum summa gravitate et moderatione honestissima fiat.

Caput 43: De his qui ad opus Dei vel ad mensam tarde occurrunt

Ad horam divini Officii, mox auditus fuerit signus, relictis omnibus quælibet fuerint in manibus, summa cum festinatione curratur, cum gravitate tamen, ut non scurrilitas inveniat fomitem. Ergo nihil operi Dei præponatur. Quod si quis in nocturnis Vigiliis post Gloriam psalmi nonagesimi quarti, quem propter hoc omnimo subtrahendo et morose volumus dici, occurrerit, non stet in ordine suo in choro, sed ultimus omnium stet aut in loco, quem talibus neglegentibus seorsum constituerit abbas, ut videantur ab ipso vel ab omnibus, usque dum conpleto opere Dei publica satisfactione pæniteat. Ideo autem eos in ultimo aut seorsum iudicavimus debere stare ut, visi ab omnibus, vel pro ipsa verecundia sua emendent; nam si foris oratorium remaneant, erit forte talis qui se aut recollocet et dormit, aut certe sedit sibi foris vel fabulis vacat, et datur occasio maligno; sed ingrediantur intus, ut nec totum perdant et de reliquo emendent. Diurnis autem Horis, qui ad opus Dei post versum et Gloriam primi psalmi qui post versum dicitur non occurrerit, lege qua supra diximus, in ultimo stent, nec præsumant sociari choro psallentium usque ad satisfactionem, nisi forte abbas licentiam dederit remissione sua, ita tamen ut satisfaciat reus ex hoc.

Ad mensam autem qui ante versu non occurrerit, ut simul omnes dicant versu et orent et sub uno omnes accedant ad mensam, qui per neglegentiam suam aut vitio non occurrerit, usque secunda vice pro hoc corripiatur; si denuo non emendaverit, non permittatur ad mensæ communis participationem, sed sequestratus a consortio omnium reficiat solus, sublata ei portione sua vinum, usque ad satisfactionem et emendationem. Similiter autem patiatur, qui et ad illum versum non fuerit præsens, qui post cibum dicitur. Et ne suis præsumat ante statutam horam vel postea quicquam cibi aut potus præsumere; sed et cui offertur aliquid a priore et accipere rennuit, hora qua desideravit

hoc quod prius recusavit aut aliud, omnimo
nihil percipiat usque emendationem congruam.

Caput 44: De his qui excommunicantur quomodo satisfaciant

Qui pro gravibus culpis ab oratorio et a mensa
excommunicantur, hora qua Opus Dei in
oratorio percelebratur, ante fores oratorii
prostratus iaceat nihil dicens, nisi tantum posito
in terra capite, status pronus omnium de
oratorio exeuntium pedibus. Et hoc tamdiu
faciat, usque dum abbas iudicaverit satisfactum
esse. Qui dum iussus ab abbate venerit, volvat
se ipsius abbatis, deinde omnium vestigiis ut
orent pro ipso. Et tunc, se iusserit abbas,
recipiatur in choro vel in ordine quo abbas
decreverit, ita sane, ut psalmum aut lectionem
vel aliud quid non præsumat in oratorio
inponere, nisi iterum abbas iubeat. Et omnibus
Horis, dum perconpletur opus Dei, proiciat se
in terra in loco qua stat. Et sic satisfaciat, usque
dum ei iubeat iterum abbas, ut quiescat iam ab
hac satisfactione. Qui vero pro levibus culpis
excommunicantur tantum a mensa, in oratorio
satisfaciant usque ad iussionem abbatis. Hoc

perficiant usque dum benedicat et dicat:
«Sufficit».

Caput 45: De his qui falluntur in oratorio

Si quis dum pronuntiat psalmum, responsorium,
antefanam vel lectionem fallitus fuerit, nisi
satisfactione ibi coram omnibus humiliatus
fuerit, maiori vindictæ subiaceat, quippe qui
noluit humilitate corrigere quod neglegentia
deliquit. Infantes autem pro tali culpa vapulent.

Caput 46: De his qui in aliis quibuslibet rebus delinquunt

Si quis dum in labore quovis, in coquina, in
cellario, in ministerio, in pistrino, in horto, in
arte aliqua dum laborat, vel in quocumque loco,
aliquid deliquerit, aut fregerit quippiam aut
perdiderit, vel aliud quid excesserit ubiubi, et
non veniens continuo ante abbatem vel
congregationem ipse ultro satisfecerit et
prodiderit delictum suum, dum per alium
cognitum fuerit, maiori subiaceat emendationi.
Si animæ vero peccati causa fuerit latens, tantum
abbati aut spiritualibus senioribus patefaciat, qui

sciat curare et sua et aliena vulnera, non detegere et publicare.

Caput 47: De significanda hora operis Dei

Nuntianda hora operis Dei dies noctisque sit cura abbatis; aut ipse nuntiare aut tali sollicito fratri iniungat hanc curam, ut omnia horis conpetentibus conpleantur. Psalmos autem vel antefanas post abbatem ordine suo quibus iussum fuerit inponant. Cantare autem et legere non præsumat, nisi qui potest ipsud officium implere ut ædificentur audientes; quod cum humilitate et gravitate et tremore fiat, et cui iusserit abbas.

Caput 48: De opera manuum cotidiana

Otiositas inimica est animæ, et ideo certis temporibus occupari debent fratres in labore manuum, certis iterum horis in lectione divina. Ideoque hac dispositione credimus utraque tempore ordinari: id est: ut a Pascha usque kalendas octobres a mane exeuntes a prima usque hora pene quarta laborent quod necessarium fuerit. Ab hora autem quarta usque hora qua Sextam agent, lectioni vacent. Post

Sextam autem surgentes a mensa pausent in lecta sua cum omni silentio, aut forte qui voluerit legere sibi sic legat, ut alium non inquietet. Et agatur Nonam temperius mediante octava hora, et iterum quod faciendum est operentur usque ad Vesperam. Si autem necessitas locis aut paupertas exegerit, ut ad fruges recollegendas per se occupentur, non contristentur. Quia tunc vere monachi sunt, si labore manuum suarum vivunt, sicut et Patres nostri et Apostoli. Omnia tamen mensurate fiant propter pusillanimes.

A kalendas autem octobres usque caput quadragesimæ usque in hora secunda plena lectioni vacent; hora secunda agatur Tertia; et usque nona omnes in opus suum laborent quod eis iniungitur. Facto autem primo signo nonæ horæ, deiungant ab opera sua singuli et sint parati, dum secundum signum pulsaverit. Post refectionem autem vacent lectionibus suis aut psalmis. In quadragesimæ vero diebus, a mane usque tertia plena vacent lectionibus suis, et usque decima hora plena operentur quod eis iniungitur. In quibus diebus quadragesimæ

dandi sunt. Ante omnia sane seputentur unus
aut duo seniores qui circumeant monasterium
horis quibus vacant fratres lectioni, et videant ne
forte inveniatur frater acediosus qui vacat otio
aut fabulis et non est intentus lectioni, et non
solum sibi inutilis est, sed etiam alios distollit.
Hic tallis si - quod absit - repertus fuerit,
corripiatur semel et secundo; si non
emendaverit, correptioni regulari subiaceat
taliter ut ceteri timeant. Neque frater ad fratrem
ingatur horis inconpetentibus.

Dominico item die lectioni vacent omnes,
excepto his qui variis officiis deputati sunt. Si
quis vero ita neglegens et desidiosus fuerit, ut
non velit aut non possit meditare aut legere,
iniungatur ei opus quod faciat, ut non vacet.
Fratribus infirmis aut delicatis talis opera aut ars
iniungatur, ut nec otiosi sint nec violentia
laboris opprimantur aut effungentur. Quorum
inbecillitas ab abbate consideranda est.

Caput 49: De quadragesimæ observatione

Licet omni tempore vita monachi quadragesimæ
debet observationem habere, tamen quia

paucorum est ista virtus, ideo suademus istis
diebus quadragesimæ omni puritate vitam suam
custodire, omnes pariter et neglegentias aliorum
temporum his diebus sanctis diluere. Quod tunc
digne fit, si ab omnibus vitiis temperamus,
orationis cum fletibus, lectioni et conpunctioni
cordis atque abstinentiæ operam damus. Ergo
his diebus augeamus nobis aliquid solito pensu
servitutis nostræ, orationes peculiares, ciborum
et potus abstinentiam, et unusquisque super
mensuram sibi indictam aliquid propria
voluntate cum gaudio Sancti Spiritus offerat
Deo, id est: subtrahat corpori suo de cibo, de
potu, de loquacitate, de scurrilitate, et cum
spiritalis desiderii gaudio sanctum Pascha
expectet. Hoc ipsud tamen quod unusquisque
offerit, abbati suo suggerat, et cum eius fiat
oratione et voluntate; quia quod sine
permissione patris spiritalis fit, præsumptioni
deputabitur et vanæ gloriæ, non mercedi. Ergo
cum voluntate abbatis omnia agenda sunt.

Caput 50: De fratribus qui longe ab oratorio laborant aut in via sunt

Fratres qui omnimo longe sunt in labore et non possunt occurrere hora conpetenti ad oratorium - et abbas hoc perpendet quia ita est - agant ibidem opus Dei, ubi operantur, cum tremore divino flectentes genua. Similiter qui in itinere directi sunt, non eos prætereant Horæ constitutæ, sed, ut possunt, agant sibi et servitutis pensum non neglegant reddere.

Caput 51: De fratribus qui non longe satis proficiscuntur

Frater qui pro quovis responso dirigitur et ea die speratur reverti ad monasterium, non præsumat foris manducare, etiam si omnimo rogetur a quovis, nisi forte ei ab abbate suo præcipiatur. Quod si aliter fecerit, excommunicetur.

Caput 52: De oratorio monasterii

Oratorium hoc sit quod dicitur, nec ibi quicquam aliud geratur aut condatur. Expleto opere Dei, omnes cum summo silentio exeant, et habeatur reverentia Deo, ut frater qui forte

sibi peculiariter vult orare, non inpediatur
alterius inprobitate. Sed et si aliter vult sibi forte
secretius orare, simpliciter intret et oret, non in
clamosa voce, sed in lacrimis et intentione
cordis. Ergo qui simile opus non facit, non
permittatur explicito opere Dei remorari in
oratorio, sicut dictum est, ne alius
impedimentum patiatur.

Caput 53: De hospitibus suscipiendis

Omnes supervenientes hospites tamquam
Christus suscipiantur, quia ipse dicturus est:
Hospis fui et suscepistis me. Et omnibus congruus
honor exhibeatur, maxime domesticis fidei et
peregrinis. Ut ergo nuntiatus fuerit hospis,
occurratur ei a priore vel a fratribus cum omni
officio caritatis; et primitus orent pariter, et sic
sibi societur in pace. Quod pacis osculum non
prius offeratur nisi oratione præmissa, propter
inlusiones diabolicas. In ipsa autem salutatione
omnis exhibeatur humilitas omnibus
venientibus sive discedentibus hospitibus:
inclinato capite vel prostrato omni corpore in
terra, Christus in eis adoretur qui et suscipitur.
Suscepti autem hospites ducantur ad orationem,

et postea sedeat cum eis prior aut cui iusserit
ipse. Legatur coram hospite Lex divina ut
ædificetur, et post hæc omnis ei exhibeatur
humanitas. Ieiunium a priore frangatur propter
hospitem, nisi forte præcipuus sit dies ieiunii qui
non possit violari; fratres autem consuetudines
ieiuniorum prosequantur. Aquam in manibus
abbas hospitibus det; pedes hospitibus omnibus
tam abbas quam cuncta congregatio lavet;
quibus lotis, hunc versum dicant: *Suscepimus,
Deus, misericordiam tuam in medio templi tui.*
Pauperum et peregrinorum maxime susceptioni
cura sollicite exhibeatur, quia in ipsis magis
Christus suscipitur; nam divitum terror ipse sibi
exigit honorem.

Coquina abbatis et hospitum super se sit, ut,
incertis horis supervenientes hospites, qui
numquam desunt monasterio, non inquietentur
fratres. In qua coquina ad annum ingrediantur
duo fratres qui ipsud officium bene impleant.
Quibus, ut indigent, solacia administrentur, ut
absque murmuratione serviant, et iterum,
quando occupationem minorem habent, exeant
ubi eis imperatur in opera. Et non solum ipsis,

sed et in omnibus officiis monasterii ista
consideratio, ut quando indigent solacia
adcommodentur eis, et iterum quando vacant
oboediant imperatis. Item et cellam hospitum
habeat adsignatam frater cuius animam timor
Dei possidet; ubi sint lecti strati sufficienter. Et
domus Dei a sapientibus administretur.
Hospitibus autem, cui non præcipitur, ullatenus
societur neque conloquatur; sed si obviaverit aut
viderit, salutatis humiliter, ut diximus, et petita
benedictione pertranseat, dicens sibi non licere
conloqui cum hospite.

Caput 54: Si debeat monachus litteras vel aliquid suscipere

Nullatenus liceat monacho neque a parentibus
suis neque a quoquam hominum nec sibi
invicem litteras, eulogias vel quælibet munuscula
accipere aut dare sine præcepto abbatis. Quod si
etiam a parentibus suis ei quicquam directum
fuerit, non præsumat suscipere illud, nisi prius
indicatum fuerit abbati. Quod si iusserit suscipi,
in abbatis sit potestate cui illud iubeat dari, et
non contristetur frater, cui forte directum
fuerat, ut non detur occasio diabulo. Qui autem

aliter præsumpserit, disciplinæ regulari
subiaceat.

Caput 55: De vestiario vel calciario fratrum

Vestimenta fratribus secundum locorum
qualitatem ubi habitant vel ærum temperiem
dentur, quia in frigidis regionibus amplius
indigetur, in calidis vero minus. Hæc ergo
consideratio penes abbatem est. Nos tamen
mediocribus locis sufficere credimus monachis
per singulos cucullam et tunicam - cucullam in
hieme vellosam, in æstate puram aut vetustam -
et scapulare propter opera, indumenta pedum
pedules et caligas. De quarum rerum omnium
colore aut grossitudine non causentur monachi,
sed quales inveniri possunt in provincia qua
degunt aut quod vilius conparari possit. Abbas
autem de mensura provideat ut non sint curta
ipsa vestimenta utentibus ea, sed mensurata.
Accipientes nova, vetera semper reddant in
præsenti reponenda in vestiario propter
pauperes. Sufficit enim monacho duas tunicas et
duas cucullas habere propter noctes et propter
lavare ipsas res; iam quod supra fuerit
superfluum est, amputari debet. Et pedules et

quodcumque est vetere reddant, dum accipiunt
novum. Femolaria hii qui in via diriguntur de
vestiario accipiant, quæ revertentes lota ibi
restituant. Et cucullæ et tunicæ sint aliquanto a
solito quas habent modice meliores; quas
exeuntes in via accipiant de vestiario et
revertentes restituant.

Stramenta autem lectorum sufficiant matta,
sagum et lena et capitale. Quæ tamen lecta
frequenter ab abbate scrutinanda sunt propter
opus peculiare, ne inveniatur. Et si cui inventum
fuerit quod ab abbate non accepit, gravissimæ
disciplinæ subiaceat. Et ut hoc vitium peculiaris
radicitus amputetur, dentur ab abbate omnia
quæ sunt necessaria: id est cuculla, tunica,
pedules, caligas, bracile, cultellum, grafium,
acum, mappula, tabulas, ut omnis auferatur
necessitatis excusatio. A quo tamen abbate
semper consideretur illa sententia Actuum
Apostolorum, quia: *Dabatur singulis prout cuique*
opus erat. Ita ergo et abbas consideret infirmitates
indigentium, non malam voluntatem
invidentium. In omnibus tamen iudiciis Dei
retributionem cogitet.

Caput 56: De mensa abbatis

Mensa abbatis cum hospitibus et peregrinis sit
semper. Quotiens tamen minus sunt hospites,
quos vult de fratribus vocare in ipsius sit
potestate. Seniorem tamen unum aut duo
semper cum fratribus dimittendum propter
disciplinam.

Caput 57: De artificibus monasterii

Artifices si sunt in monasterio cum omni
humilitate faciant ipsas artes, si permiserit
abbas. Quod si aliquis ex eis extollitur pro
scientiæ artis suæ, eo quod videatur aliquid
conferre monasterio, hic talis erigatur ab ipsa
arte et denuo per eam non transeat, nisi forte
humiliato ei iterum abbas iubeat. Si quid vero ex
operibus artificum venundandum est, videant
ipsi per quorum manum transigendam sint, ne
aliquam fraudem præsumant. Memorentur
semper Ananiæ et Safiræ, ne forte mortem
quam illi in corpore pertulerunt, hanc isti vel
omnes qui aliquam fraudem de rebus monasterii
fecerint, in anima patiantur. In ipsis autem
pretiis non subripiat avaritiæ malum, sed semper

aliquantulum vilius detur quam ab aliis
sæcularibus dari potest, ut in omnibus
glorificetur Deus.

Caput 58: De disciplina suscipiendorum fratrum

Noviter veniens quis ad conversationem, non ei
facilis tribuatur ingressus, sed sicut ait
Apostolus: *Probate spiritus si ex Deo sunt.* Ergo si
veniens perseveraverit pulsans et inlatas sibi
iniurias et difficultatem ingressus post quattuor
aut quinque dies visus fuerit patienter portare et
persistere petitioni suæ, annuatur ei ingressus et
sit in cella hospitum paucis diebus. Postea
autem sit in cella noviciorum ubi meditent et
manducent et dormiant. Et senior eis talis
deputetur qui aptus sit ad lucrandas animas, qui
super eos omnimo curiose intendat. Et
sollicitudo sit si revera Deum quærit, si sollicitus
est ad opus Dei, ad oboedientiam, ad obprobria.
Prædicentur ei omnia dura et aspera per quæ
itur ad Deum. Si promiserit de stabilitatis suæ
perseverentia, post duorum mensuum circulum
legatur ei hæc regula per ordinem, et dicatur ei:
«Ecce lex sub qua militare vis; si potes

observare, ingredere; si vero non potes, liber discede». Si adhuc steterit, tunc ducatur in supradictam cellam noviciorum et iterum probetur in omni patientia. Et post sex mensuum circuitum legatur ei regula, ut sciat ad quod ingreditur. Et si adhuc stat, post quattuor menses iterum relegatur ei eadem regula. Et si habita secum deliberatione promiserit se omnia custodire et cuncta sibi imperata servare, tunc suscipiatur in congregatione, sciens et lege regulæ constitutum quod ei ex illa die non liceat egredi monasterio, nec collum excutere de sub iugo regulæ quem sub tam morosam deliberationem licuit aut excusare aut suscipere.

Suscipiendus autem in oratorio coram omnibus promittat de stabilitate sua et conversatione morum suorum et oboedientia, coram Deo et sanctis eius, ut si aliquando aliter fecerit, ab eo se damnandum sciat quem inridit. De qua promissione sua faciat petitionem ad nomen sanctorum quorum reliquiæ ibi sunt et abbatis præsentis. Quam petitionem manu sua scribat, aut certe, si non scit litteras, alter ab eo rogatus scribat et ille novicius signum faciat et manu sua eam super altare ponat. Quam dum inposuerit, incipiat ipse novicius mox hunc versum: *Suscipe me, Domine, secundum eloquium tuum et vivam, et ne confundas me ab expectatione mea.* Quem versum omnis congregatio tertio respondeat, adiungentes: Gloria Patri. Tunc ille frater novicius prosternatur singulorum pedibus ut orent pro eo; et iam ex illa die in congregatione reputetur. Res si quas habet, aut eroget prius pauperibus aut facta sollemniter donatione conferat monasterio, nihil sibi reservans ex omnibus, quippe qui ex illo die nec proprii corporis potestatem se habiturum scit. Mox ergo in oratorio exuatur rebus propriis quibus vestitus est, et induatur rebus monasterii. Illa autem vestimenta quibus exutus est reponatur in vestiario conservanda, ut si aliquando suadenti diabulo consenserit ut egrediatur de monasterio - quod absit - tunc exutus rebus monasterii proiciatur. Illam tamen petitionem eius, quam desuper altare abbas tulit, non recipiat, sed in monasterio reservetur.

Caput 59: De filiis nobilium aut pauperum qui offeruntur

Si quis forte de nobilibus offerit filium suum Deo in monasterio, si ipse puer minor ætate est, parentes eius faciant petitionem quam supra diximus, et cum oblatione ipsam petitionem et manum pueri involvant in palla altaris, et sic eum offerant. De rebus autem suis aut in præsenti petitione promittant sub iureiurando, quia numquam per se, numquam per suffectam personam nec quolibet modo ei aliquando aliquid dant aut tribuunt occasionem habendi; vel certe si hoc facere noluerint et aliquid offere volunt in elemosinam monasterio pro mercede sua, faciant ex rebus quas dare volunt monasterio donationem, reservato sibi, si ita voluerint usum fructum. Atque ita omnia obstruantur ut nulla suspicio remaneat puero per quam deceptus perire possit - quod absit - quod experimento didicimus. Similiter autem et pauperiores faciant. Qui vero ex toto nihil habent, simpliciter petitionem faciant et cum oblatione offerant filium suum coram testibus.

Caput 60: De sacerdotibus qui forte voluerint in monasterio habitare

Si quis de ordine sacerdotum in monasterio se suscipi rogaverit, non quidem citius ei adsentiatur. Tamen, si omnimo persteterit in hac supplicatione, sciat se omnem regulæ disciplinam servaturum, nec aliquid ei relaxabitur, ut sicut scriptum est: *Amice, ad quod venisti?* Concedatur ei tamen post abbatem stare et benedicere aut missas tenere, si tamen iusserit ei abbas. Sin alias, ullatenus aliqua præsumat, sciens se disciplinæ regulari subditum, et magis humilitatis exempla omnibus det. Et si forte ordinationis aut alicuius rei causa fuerit in monasterio, illum locum adtendat quando ingressus est in monasterio, non illum qui ei pro reverentia sacerdotii concessus est. Clericorum autem si quis eodem desiderio monasterio sociari voluerit, loco mediocri conlocentur; et ipsi tamen si promittunt de observatione regulæ vel propria stabilitate.

Caput 61: De monachis peregrinis qualiter suscipiantur

Si quis monachus peregrinus de longiquis provinciis supervenerit, si pro hospite voluerit habitare in monasterio et contentus fuerit consuetudinem loci quam invenerit, et non forte superfluitate sua perturbat monasterium, sed simpliciter contentus est quod invenerit, suscipiatur quanto tempore cupit. Si qua sane rationabiliter et cum humilitate caritatis reprehendit aut ostendit, tractet abbas prudenter ne forte pro hoc ipsud eum Dominus direxerit. Si vero postea voluerit stabilitatem suam firmare, non rennuatur talis voluntas, et maxime quia tempore hospitalitatis potuit eius vita dinosci.

Quod si superfluus aut vitiosus inventus fuerit tempore hospitalitatis, non solum non debet sociari corpori monasterii, verum etiam dicatur ei honeste ut discedat, ne eius miseria etiam alii vitientur. Quod si non fuerit talis qui mereatur proici, non solum si petierit, suscipiatur congregationi sociandus, verum etiam suadeatur ut stet, ut eius exemplo alii erudiantur, et quia in

omni loco uni Domino servitur, uni Regi
militatur. Quem si etiam talem esse perspexerit
abbas, liceat eum in superiori aliquantum
constituere loco. Non solum autem monachum,
sed etiam de suprascriptis gradibus sacerdotum
vel clericorum stabilire potest abbas in maiori
quam ingrediuntur loco, si eorum talem
perspexerit esse vitam. Caveat autem abbas, ne
aliquando de alio noto monasterio monachum
ad habitandum suscipiat sine consensu abbatis
eius aut litteras commendaticias, quia scriptum
est: *Quod tibi non vis fieri, alio ne feceris.*

Caput 62: De sacerdotibus monasterii

Si quis abbas sibi presbyterum vel diaconem
ordinari petierit, de suis elegat qui dignus sit
sacerdotio fungi. Ordinatus autem caveat
elationem aut superbiam, nec quicquam
præsumat nisi quod ei ab abbate præcipitur,
sciens se multo magis disciplinæ regulari
subdendum. Nec occasione sacerdotii
obliviscatur regulæ oboedientiam et disciplinam
sed magis ac magis in Deum proficiat. Locum
vero illum semper adtendat quod ingressus est
in monasterio, præter officium altaris, et si forte

electio congregationis et voluntas abbatis pro
vitæ merito eum promovere voluerint. Qui
tamen regulam decanis vel præpositis
constitutam sibi servare sciat. Quod si aliter
præsumpserit, non sacerdos sed rebellio
iudicetur. Et sæpe admonitus si non correxerit,
etiam episcopus adhibeatur in testimonio. Quod
si nec sic emendaverit, clarescentibus culpis,
proiciatur de monasterio, si tamen talis fuerit
eius contumacia ut subdi aut oboedire regulæ
nolit.

Caput 63: De ordine congregationis

Ordines suos in monasterio ita conservent ut
conversationis tempus, ut vitæ meritum
discernit atque abbas constituerit. Qui abbas
non conturbet gregem sibi commissum nec,
quasi libera utens potestate, iniuste disponat
aliquid, sed cogitet semper quia de omnibus
iudiciis et operibus suis redditurus est Deo
rationem. Ergo secundum ordines suos quos
constituerit vel quos habuerint ipsi fratres, sic
accedant ad pacem, ad communionem, ad
psalmum inponendum, in choro standum. Et in
omnibus omnimo locis ætas non discernat

ordines nec præiudicet, quia Samuhel et Danihel
pueri presbyteros iudicaverunt. Ergo, excepto
hos quos, ut diximus, altiori consilio abbas
prætulerit vel degradaverit certis ex causis,
reliqui omnes ut convertuntur ita sint ut verbi
gratia qui secunda hora diei venerit in
monasterio iuniorem se noverit illius esse qui
prima hora venit diei, cuiuslibet ætatis aut
dignitatis sit. Pueris per omnia ab omnibus
disciplina conservata.

Iuniores igitur priores suos honorent, priores
minores suos diligant. In ipsa appellatione
nominum nulli liceat alium puro appellare
nomine, sed proiores iuniores suos fratrum
nomine, iuniores autem priores suos nonnos
vocent, quod intelligitur paterna reverentia.
Abbas autem, quia vices Christi creditur agere,
dominus et abbas vocetur, non sua adsumptione
sed honore et amore Christi; ipse autem cogitet
et sic se exhibeat ut dignus sit tali honore.
Ubicumque autem sibi obviant fratres, iunior
priorem benedictionem petat. Transeunte
maiore minor surgat et det ei locum sedendi,
nec præsumat iunior consedere nisi ei præcipiat

senior suus, ut fiat quod scriptum est: *Honore
invicem prævenientes*. Pueri parvi vel adulescentes
in oratorio vel ad mensas cum disciplina ordines
suos consequantur. Foris autem vel ubiubi, et
custodiam habeant et disciplinam, usque dum
ad intellegibilem ætatem perveniant.

Caput 64: De ordinando abbate

In abbatis ordinatione illa semper consideretur
ratio, ut hic constituatur quem sibi omnis
concors congregatio secundum timorem Dei,
sive etiam pars quamvis parva congregationis
saniore consilio elegerit. Vitæ autem merito et
sapientiæ doctrina elegatur qui ordinandus est,
etiam si ultimus fuerit in ordine congregationis.
Quod si etiam omnis congregatio vitiis suis -
quod quidem absit - consentientem personam
pari consilio elegerit, et vitia ipsa aliquatenus in
notitia episcopi ad cuius diocesim pertinet locus
ipse vel ab abbates aut christianos vicinos
claruerint, prohibeant pravorum prævalere
consensum, sed domui Dei dignum constituant
dispensatorem, scientes pro hoc se recepturos
mercedem bonam, si illud caste et zelo Dei
faciant, sicut e diverso peccatum si neglegant.

Ordinatus autem abbas cogitet semper, quale
onus suscepit et cui redditurus est rationem
vilicationis suæ, sciatque sibi oportere prodesse
magis quam præesse. Oportet ergo eum esse
doctum Lege divina, ut sciat et si unde proferat
nova et vetera, castum, sobrium, misericordem,
et semper superexaltet misericordiam iudicio, ut
idem ipse consequatur. Oderit vitia, diligat
fratres. In ipsa autem correptione prudenter
agat et ne quid nimis, ne dum nimis eradere
cupit æruginem frangatur vas. Suamque
fragilitatem semper suspectus sit, memineritque
calamum quassatum non conterendum. In
quibus non dicimus ut permittat nutriri vitia, sed
prudenter et cum caritate ea amputet, ut viderit
cuique expedire sicut iam diximus, et studeat
plus amari quam timeri. Non sit turbulentus et
anxius, non sit nimius et obstinatus, non sit
zelotipus et nimis suspiciosus, quia numquam
requiescit. In ipsis imperiis suis providus et
consideratus, et sive secundum Deum sive
secundum sæculum sit opera quam iniungit,
discernat et temperet, cogitans discretionem
sancti Iacob dicentis: *Si gerges meos plus in
ambulando fecero laborare, morientur cuncti una die.*

Hæc ergo aliaque testimonia discretionis matris
virtutum sumens, sic omnia temperet ut sit et
fortes quod cupiant et infirmi non refugiant. Et
præcipue ut præsentem regulam in omnibus
conservet, ut dum bene ministraverit audiat a
Domino quod servus bonus qui erogavit
triticum conservis in tempore suo: *Amen dico
vobis, ait, super omnia bona sua constituit eum.*

Caput 65: De præposito monasterii

Sæpius quidem contigit, ut per ordinationem
præpositi sandala gravia in monasteriis oriantur,
dum sint aliqui maligno spiritu superbiæ inflati
et æstimantes se secundos esse abbates,
adsumentes sibi tyrannidem, scandala nutriunt
et dissensiones in congregationes faciunt, et
maxime in illis locis ubi ab eodem sacerdote vel
ab eis abbatibus qui abbatem ordinant ab ipsis
etiam et præpositus ordinatur. Quod quam sit
absurdum facile advertitur, quia ab ipso initio
ordinationis materia ei datur superbiendi, dum
ei suggeritur a cogitationibus suis exutum eum
esse a potestate abbatis sui, quia ab ipsis es tu
ordinatus a quibus et abbas. Hinc suscitantur
invidiæ, rixæ, detractiones, æmulationes,

dissensiones, exordinationes, ut dum contraria
sibi abbas præpositusque sentiunt, et ipsorum
necesse est sub hanc dissensionem animas
periclitari, et hii qui sub ipsi sunt, dum adulantur
partibus, eunt in perditionem. Cuius periculi
malum illos respicit in capite qui talius
inordinationis se fecerunt auctores.

Ideo nos vidimus expedire propter pacis
caritatisque custodiam in abbatis pendere
arbitrio ordinationem monasterii sui. Et si
potest fieri per decanos ordinetur, ut ante
disposuimus, omnis utilitas monasterii, prout
abbas disposuerit, ut dum pluribus committitur,
unus non superbiat. Quod si aut locus expetit
aut congregatio petierit rationabiliter cum
humilitate et abbas iudicaverit expedire,
quemcumque elegerit abbas cum consilio
fratrum timentium Deum ordinet ipse sibi
præpositum. Qui tamen præpositus illa agat cum
reverentia quæ ab abbate suo et iniuncta fuerint,
nihil contra abbatis voluntatem aut
ordinationem faciens, quia quantum prælatus est
ceteris, ita eum oportet sollicitius observare
præcepta regulæ. Qui præpositus si repertus

fuerit vitiosus aut elatione deceptus superbire,
aut contemptor sanctæ regulæ fuerit
conprobatus, admoneatur verbis usque quater.
Si non emendaverit, adhibeatur ei correptio
disciplinæ regularis. Quod si neque sic
correxerit, tunc deiciatur de ordine præposituræ
et alius qui dignus est in loco eius subrogetur.
Quod si et postea in congregatione quietus et
oboediens non fuerit, etiam de monasterio
pellatur. Cogitet tamen abbas se de omnibus
iudiciis suis Deo reddere rationem, ne forte
invidiæ aut zeli flamma urat animam.

Caput 66: De hostiariis monasterii

Ad portam monasterii ponatur senes sapiens,
qui sciat accipere responsum et reddere, et cuius
maturitas eum non sinat vacari. Qui portarius
cellam debebit habere iuxta portam, ut
venientes semper præsentem inveniant a quo
responsum accipiant. Et mox ut aliquis
pulsaverit aut pauper clamaverit, «Deo gratias»
respondeat aut «Benedic», et cum omni
mansuetudine timoris Dei reddat responsum
festinanter cum fervore caritatis. Qui portarius
si indiget solacio iuniorem fratrem accipiat.

Monasterium autem, si possit fieri, ita debet
constitui ut omnia necessaria, id est aqua,
molendinum, hortum vel artes diversas intra
monasterium exerceantur, ut non sit necessitas
monachis vagandi foris, quia omnimo non
expedit animabus eorum.Hanc autem regulam
sæpius volumus in congregatione legi, ne quis
fratrum se de ignorantia excuset.

Caput 67: De fratribus in viam directis

Dirigendi fratres in via omnium fratrum vel
abbatis se orationi conmendent, et semper ad
orationem ultimam operis Dei commemoratio
omnium absentum fiat. Revertentes autem de
via fratres ipso die quo redeunt per omnes
canonicas horas, dum expletur opus Dei,
prostrati solo oratorii ab omnibus petant
orationem propter excessos, ne qui forte
subripuerint in via visus aut auditus malæ rei aut
otiosi sermonis. Nec præsumat quisquam
referre alio quæcumque foris monasterium
viderit aut audierit, quia plurima destructio est.
Quod si quis præsumpserit, vindictæ regulari
subiaceat. Similiter et qui præsumpserit claustra
monasterii egredi vel quocumque ire vel

quippiam quamvis parvum sine iussione abbatis
facere.

Caput 68: Si fratri inpossibilia iniungantur

Si cui fratri aliqua forte gravia aut inpossibilia
iniunguntur suscipiat quidem iubentis imperium
cum omni mansuetudine et oboedientia. Quod
si omnimo virium suarum mensuram viderit
pondus oneris excedere, inpossibilitatis suæ
causas ei qui sibi præest patienter et oportune
suggerat, non superbiendo aut resistendo vel
contradicendo. Quod si post suggestionem
suam in sua sententia prioris imperium
perduraverit, sciat iunior ita sibi expedire, et ex
caritate, confidens de adiutorio Dei, oboediat.

Caput 69: Ut in monasterio non præsumat
alter alterum defendere

Præcavendum est ne quavis occasione præsumat
alter alium defendere monachum in monasterio
aut quasi tueri, etiam si qualivis consanguinitatis
propinquitate iungantur. Nec quolibet modo id
a monachis præsumatur, quia exinde gravissima
occasio scandalorum oriri potest. Quod si quis
hæc transgressus fuerit, acrius coerceatur.

Caput 70: Ut non præsumat passim aliquis cædere

Vitetur in monasterio omnis præsumptionis occasio; atque constituimus ut nulli liceat quemquam fratrum suorum excommunicare aut cædere, nisi cui potestas ab abbate date fuerit. Peccantes autem coram omnibus arguantur ut ceteri metum habeant. Infantum vero usque quindecim annorum ætates disciplinæ diligentia ab omnibus et custodia sit; sed et hoc cum omni mensura et ratione. Nam in fortiori ætate qui præsumit aliquatenus sine præcepto abbatis vel in ipsis infantibus sine discretione exarserit, disciplinæ regulari subiaceat, quia scriptum est: *Quod tibi non vis fieri, alio ne feceris.*

Caput 71: Ut oboedientes sibi sint invicem

Oboedientiæ bonum non solum abbati exhibendum est ab omnibus, sed etiam sibi invicem ita oboediant fratres, scientes per hanc oboedientiæ viam se ituros ad Deum. Præmisso ergo abbatis aut præpositorum qui ab eo constituuntur imperio, cui non permittimus privata imperia præponi, de cetero omnes

iuniores prioribus suis omni caritate et
sollicitudine oboediant. Quod si quis
contentiosus repperitur, corripiatur. Si quis
autem frater pro quavis minima causa ab abbate
vel a quocumque priore corripitur quolibet
modo, vel si leviter senserit animos prioris
cuiuscumque contra se iratos vel commotos
quamvis modice, mox sine mora tamdiu
prostratus in terra ante pedes eius iaceat
satisfaciens, usque dum benedictione sanetur illa
commotio. Quod si contempserit facere, aut
corporali vindictæ subiaceat aut, si contumax
fuerit, de monasterio expellatur.

Caput 72: De zelo bono quod debent monachi habere

Sicut est zelus amaritudinis malus qui separat a
Deo et ducit ad infernum, ita est zelus bonus
qui separat a vitia et ducit ad Deum et ad vitam
æternam. Hunc ergo zelum ferventissimo amore
exerceant monachi, id est ut honore se invicem
præveniant, infirmitates suas sive corporum sive
morum patientissime tolerent, oboedientiam
sibi certatim inpendant: nullus quod sibi utile
iudicat sequatur, sed quod magis alio; caritatem

fraternitatis caste inpendant. Amore Deum
timeant. Abbatem suum sincera et humili
caritate diligant. Christo omnimo nihil
præponant, qui nos pariter ad vitam æternam
perducat.

Caput 73: De hoc quod non omnis iustitiæ observatio in hac sit regula constituta

Regulam autem hanc descripsimus, Regulam
autem hanc descripsimus, ut hanc observantes
in monasteriis aliquatenus vel honestatem
morum aut initium conversationis nos
demonstremus habere. Ceterum ad
perfectionem conversationis qui festinat, sunt
doctrinæ sanctorum Patrum, quarum observatio
perducat hominem ad celsitudinem perfectionis.
Quæ enim pagina aut qui sermo divinæ
auctoritatis Veteris ac Novi Testamenti non est
rectissima norma vitæ humanæ? Aut quis liber
sanctorum catholicorum Patrum hoc non
resonat ut recto cursu perveniamus ad
Creatorem nostrum? Necnon et Collationes
Patrum et Instituta et Vitas eorum, sed et regula
sancti Patris nostri Basilii, quid aliud sunt nisi
bene viventium et oboedientium monachorum

instrumenta virtutum? Nobis autem desidiosis et male viventibus atque neglegentibus rubor confusionis est. Quisquis ergo ad patriam cælestem festinas, hanc minimam inchoationis regulam descriptam adiuvante Christo perfice; et tunc demum ad maiora, quæ supra commemoravimus, doctrinæ virtutumque culmina Deo protegente pervenies. Amen.